Shriga V.

THE PELICAN SHAKESPEARE
GENERAL EDITORS

STEPHEN ORGEL
A. R. BRAUNMULLER

A Midsummer Night's Dream

The feuding Oberon and Titania meet by moonlight,
mirroring the loving enemies Theseus and Hippolyta.
Frontispiece to the play in Nicholas Rowe's Shakespeare, 1709,
the first illustrated edition. The play was performed during the
Restoration in various fragmentary forms, culminating in 1692
with *The Fairy Queen,* an anonymous adaptation with
magnificent music by Purcell. The costumes are those
of the early-eighteenth-century stage.

William Shakespeare

————

A Midsummer Night's Dream

EDITED BY RUSS McDONALD

PENGUIN BOOKS

PENGUIN BOOKS

Published by the Penguin Group

Penguin Group (USA) Inc., 375 Hudson Street, New York, New York 10014, U.S.A.

Penguin Group (Canada), 90 Eglinton Avenue East, Suite 700, Toronto,
Ontario, Canada M4P 2Y3 (a division of Pearson Penguin Canada Inc.)

Penguin Books Ltd, 80 Strand, London WC2R 0RL, England

Penguin Ireland, 25 St Stephen's Green, Dublin 2, Ireland (a division of Penguin Books Ltd)

Penguin Group (Australia), 250 Camberwell Road, Camberwell,
Victoria 3124, Australia (a division of Pearson Australia Group Pty Ltd)

Penguin Books India Pvt Ltd, 11 Community Centre, Panchsheel Park, New Delhi – 110 017, India

Penguin Group (NZ), cnr Airborne and Rosedale Roads,
Albany, Auckland 1310, New Zealand (a division of Pearson New Zealand Ltd)

Penguin Books (South Africa) (Pty) Ltd, 24 Sturdee Avenue,
Rosebank, Johannesburg 2196, South Africa

Penguin Books Ltd, Registered Offices: 80 Strand, London WC2R 0RL, England

A Midsummer Night's Dream edited by Madeleine Doran published
in the United States of America in
Penguin Books 1959
Revised edition published 1971
This new edition edited by Russ McDonald published 2000

20 19 18 17 16 15 14 13 12 11

ISBN 0-14-07.1455 3
(CIP data available)
Printed in the United States of America
Set in Adobe Garamond
Designed by Virginia Norey

Contents

Publisher's Note

IT IS ALMOST half a century since the first volumes of the Pelican Shakespeare appeared under the general editorship of Alfred Harbage. The fact that a new edition, rather than simply a revision, has been undertaken reflects the profound changes textual and critical studies of Shakespeare have undergone in the past twenty years. For the new Pelican series, the texts of the plays and poems have been thoroughly revised in accordance with recent scholarship, and in some cases have been entirely reedited. New introductions and notes have been provided in all the volumes. But the new Shakespeare is also designed as a successor to the original series; the previous editions have been taken into account, and the advice of the previous editors has been solicited where it was feasible to do so.

Certain textual features of the new Pelican Shakespeare should be particularly noted. All lines are numbered that contain a word, phrase, or allusion explained in the glossarial notes. In addition, for convenience, every tenth line is also numbered, in italics when no annotation is indicated. The intrusive and often inaccurate place headings inserted by early editors are omitted (as is becoming standard practice), but for the convenience of those who miss them, an indication of locale now appears as the first item in the annotation of each scene.

In the interest of both elegance and utility, each speech prefix is set in a separate line when the speaker's lines are in verse, except when those words form the second half of a verse line. Thus the verse form of the speech is kept visually intact. What is printed as verse and what is printed as prose has, in general, the authority of the original texts. Departures from the original texts in this regard have only the authority of editorial tradition and the judgment of the Pelican editors; and, in a few instances, are admittedly arbitrary.

The Theatrical World

Economic realities determined the theatrical world in which Shakespeare's plays were written, performed, and received. For centuries in England, the primary theatrical tradition was nonprofessional. Craft guilds (or "mysteries") provided religious drama – mystery plays – as part of the celebration of religious and civic festivals, and schools and universities staged classical and neoclassical drama in both Latin and English as part of their curricula. In these forms, drama was established and socially acceptable. Professional theater, in contrast, existed on the margins of society. The acting companies were itinerant; playhouses could be any available space – the great halls of the aristocracy, town squares, civic halls, inn yards, fair booths, or open fields – and income was sporadic, dependent on the passing of the hat or on the bounty of local patrons. The actors, moreover, were considered little better than vagabonds, constantly in danger of arrest or expulsion.

In the late 1560s and 1570s, however, English professional theater began to gain respectability. Wealthy aristocrats fond of drama – the Lord Admiral, for example, or the Lord Chamberlain – took acting companies under their protection so that the players technically became members of their households and were no longer subject to arrest as homeless or masterless men. Permanent theaters were first built at this time as well, allowing the companies to control and charge for entry to their performances.

Shakespeare's livelihood, and the stunning artistic explosion in which he participated, depended on pragmatic and architectural effort. Professional theater requires ways to restrict access to its offerings; if it does not, and admission fees cannot be charged, the actors do not get paid, the costumes go to a pawnbroker, and there is no such thing as a professional, ongoing theatrical tradition. The answer to that economic need arrived in the late 1560s and 1570s with the creation of the so-called public or amphitheater playhouse. Recent discoveries indicate that the precursor of the Globe playhouse in London (where Shakespeare's mature plays were presented) and the Rose theater (which presented Christopher Marlowe's plays and some of Shakespeare's earliest ones) was the Red Lion theater of 1567. Archaeological studies of the foundations of the Rose and Globe theaters have revealed that the open-air theater of the 1590s and later was probably a polygonal building with fourteen to twenty or twenty-four sides, multistoried, from 75 to 100 feet in diameter, with a raised, partly covered "thrust" stage that projected into a group of standing patrons, or "groundlings," and a covered gallery, seating up to 2,500 or more (very crowded) spectators.

These theaters might have been about half full on any given day, though the audiences were larger on holidays or when a play was advertised, as old and new were, through printed playbills posted around London. The metropolitan area's late-Tudor, early-Stuart population (circa 1590–1620) has been estimated at about 150,000 to 250,000. It has been supposed that in the mid-1590s there were about 15,000 spectators per week at the public theaters; thus, as many as 10 percent of the local population went to the theater regularly. Consequently, the theaters' repertories – the plays available for this experienced and frequent audience – had to change often: in the month between September 15 and October 15, 1595, for instance, the Lord Admiral's Men performed twenty-eight times in eighteen different plays.

Since natural light illuminated the amphitheaters' stages, performances began between noon and two o'clock and ran without a break for two or three hours. They often concluded with a jig, a fencing display, or some other nondramatic exhibition. Weather conditions determined the season for the amphitheaters: plays were performed every day (including Sundays, sometimes, to clerical dismay) except during Lent – the forty days before Easter – or periods of plague, or sometimes during the summer months when law courts were not in session and the most affluent members of the audience were not in London.

To a modern theatergoer, an amphitheater stage like that of the Rose or Globe would appear an unfamiliar mixture of plainness and elaborate decoration. Much of the structure was carved or painted, sometimes to imitate marble; elsewhere, as under the canopy projecting over the stage, to represent the stars and the zodiac. Appropriate painted canvas pictures (of Jerusalem, for example, if the play was set in that city) were apparently hung on the wall behind the acting area, and tragedies were accompanied by black hangings, presumably something like crepe festoons or bunting. Although these theaters did not employ what we would call scenery, early modern spectators saw numerous large props, such as the "bar" at which a prisoner stood during a trial, the "mossy bank" where lovers reclined, an arbor for amorous conversation, a chariot, gallows, tables, trees, beds, thrones, writing desks, and so forth. Audiences might learn a scene's location from a sign (reading "Athens," for example) carried across the stage (as in Bertolt Brecht's twentieth-century productions). Equally captivating (and equally irritating to the theater's enemies) were the rich costumes and personal props the actors used: the most valuable items in the surviving theatrical inventories are the swords, gowns, robes, crowns, and other items worn or carried by the performers.

Magic appealed to Shakespeare's audiences as much as it does to us today, and the theater exploited many deceptive and spectacular devices. A winch in the loft above the stage, called "the heavens," could lower and raise actors playing gods, goddesses, and other supernatural figures to and from the main acting area, just as one or more trapdoors permitted entrances and exits to and from the area, called "hell," beneath the stage. Actors wore elementary makeup such as wigs, false beards, and face paint, and they employed pig's bladders filled with animal blood to make wounds seem more real. They had rudimentary but effective ways of pretending to behead or hang a person. Supernumeraries (stagehands or actors not needed in a particular scene) could make thunder sounds (by shaking a metal sheet or rolling an iron ball down a chute) and show lightning (by blowing inflammable resin through tubes into a flame). Elaborate fireworks enhanced the effects of dragons flying through the air or imitated such celestial phenomena as comets, shooting stars, and multiple suns. Horses' hoofbeats, bells (located perhaps in the tower above the stage), trumpets and drums, clocks, cannon shots and gunshots, and the like were common sound effects. And the music of viols, cornets, oboes, and recorders was a regular feature of theatrical performances.

For two relatively brief spans, from the late 1570s to 1590 and from 1599 to 1614, the amphitheaters competed with the so-called private, or indoor, theaters, which originated as, or later represented themselves as, educational institutions training boys as singers for church services and court performances. These indoor theaters had two features that were distinct from the amphitheaters': their personnel and their playing spaces. The amphitheaters' adult companies included both adult men, who played the male roles, and boys, who played the female roles; the private, or indoor, theater companies, on the other hand, were entirely composed of boys aged about 8 to 16, who were, or could pretend to be, candidates for singers in a church or a royal boys' choir. (Until 1660, professional theatrical companies included no women.) The playing space would appear much more familiar to modern audiences than the long-vanished amphitheaters; the later indoor theaters were, in fact, the ancestors of the typical modern theater. They were enclosed spaces, usually rectangular, with the stage filling one end of the rectangle and the audience arrayed in seats or benches across (and sometimes lining) the building's longer axis. These spaces staged plays less frequently than the public theaters (perhaps only once a week) and held far fewer spectators than the amphitheaters: about 200 to 600, as opposed to 2,500 or more. Fewer patrons mean a smaller gross income, unless each pays more. Not surprisingly, then, private theaters charged higher prices than the amphitheaters, probably sixpence, as opposed to a penny for the cheapest entry.

Protected from the weather, the indoor theaters presented plays later in the day than the amphitheaters, and used artificial illumination – candles in sconces or candelabra. But candles melt, and need replacing, snuffing, and trimming, and these practical requirements may have been part of the reason the indoor theaters introduced breaks in the performance, the intermission so dear to the heart of theatergoers and to the pocketbooks of theater concessionaires ever since. Whether motivated by the need to tend to the candles or by the entrepreneurs' wishing to sell oranges and liquor, or both, the indoor theaters eventually established the modern convention of the non-continuous performance. In the early modern "private" theater, musical performances apparently filled the intermissions, which in Stuart theater jargon seem to have been called "acts."

At the end of the first decade of the seventeenth century, the distinction between public amphitheaters and private indoor companies ceased. For various cultural, political, and economic reasons, individual companies gained control of both the public, open-air theaters and the indoor ones, and companies mixing adult men and boys took over the formerly "private" theaters. Despite the death of the boys' companies and of their highly innovative theaters (for which such luminous playwrights as Ben Jonson, George Chapman, and John Marston wrote), their playing spaces and conventions had an immense impact on subsequent plays: not merely for the intervals (which stressed the artistic and architectonic importance of "acts"), but also because they introduced political and social satire as a popular dramatic ingredient, even in tragedy, and a wider range of actorly effects, encouraged by their more intimate playing spaces.

Even the briefest sketch of the Shakespearean theatrical world would be incomplete without some comment on the social and cultural dimensions of theaters and playing in the period. In an intensely hierarchical and status-conscious society, professional actors and their ventures had hardly any respectability; as we have indicated, to protect themselves against laws designed to curb vagabondage and the increase of masterless men, actors resorted to the near-fiction that they were the servants of noble masters, and wore their distinctive livery. Hence the company for which Shakespeare wrote in the 1590s called itself the Lord Chamberlain's Men and pretended that the public, money-getting performances were in fact rehearsals for private performances before that high court official. From 1598, the Privy Council had licensed theatrical companies, and after 1603, with the accession of King James I, the companies gained explicit royal protection, just as the Queen's Men had for a time under Queen Elizabeth. The Chamberlain's Men became the King's Men, and the other companies were patronized by the other members of the royal family.

These designations were legal fictions that half-concealed an important economic and social development, the evolution away from the theater's organization on the model of the guild, a self-regulating confraternity of individual artisans, into a proto-capitalist organization. Shakespeare's company became a joint-stock company, where persons who supplied capital and, in some cases, such as Shakespeare's, capital and talent, employed themselves and others in earning a return on that capital. This development meant that actors and theater companies were outside both the traditional guild structures, which required some form of civic or royal charter, and the feudal household organization of master-and-servant. This anomalous, maverick social and economic condition made theater companies practically unruly and potentially even dangerous; consequently, numerous official bodies – including the London metropolitan and ecclesiastical authorities as well as, occasionally, the royal court itself – tried, without much success, to control and even to disband them.

Public officials had good reason to want to close the theaters: they were attractive nuisances – they drew often riotous crowds, they were always noisy, and they could be politically offensive and socially insubordinate. Until the Civil War, however, anti-theatrical forces failed to shut down professional theater, for many reasons – limited surveillance and few police powers, tensions or outright hostilities among the agencies that sought to check or channel theatrical activity, and lack of clear policies for control. Another reason must have been the theaters' undeniable popularity. Curtailing any activity enjoyed by such a substantial percentage of the population was difficult, as various Roman emperors attempting to limit circuses had learned, and the Tudor-Stuart audience was not merely large, it was socially diverse and included women. The prevalence of public entertainment in this period has been underestimated. In fact, fairs, holidays, games, sporting events, the equivalent of modern parades, freak shows, and street exhibitions all abounded, but the theater was the most widely and frequently available entertainment to which people of every class had access. That fact helps account both for its quantity and for the fear and anger it aroused.

WILLIAM SHAKESPEARE OF
STRATFORD-UPON-AVON, GENTLEMAN

Many people have said that we know very little about William Shakespeare's life – pinheads and postcards are often mentioned as appropriately tiny surfaces on which to record the available information. More imaginatively and perhaps more correctly, Ralph Waldo Emerson wrote, "Shakespeare is the only biographer of Shakespeare. . . . So far from Shakespeare's being the least known, he is the one person in all modern history fully known to us."

In fact, we know more about Shakespeare's life than we do about almost any other English writer's of his era. His last will and testament (dated March 25, 1616) survives, as do numerous legal contracts and court documents involving Shakespeare as principal or witness, and parish records in Stratford and London. Shakespeare appears quite often in official records of King James's royal court, and of course Shakespeare's name appears on numerous title pages and in the written and recorded words of his literary contemporaries Robert Greene, Henry Chettle, Francis Meres, John Davies of Hereford, Ben Jonson, and many others. Indeed, if we make due allowance for the bloating of modern, run-of-the-mill bureaucratic records, more information has survived over the past four hundred years about William Shakespeare of Stratford-upon-Avon, Warwickshire, than is likely to survive in the next four hundred years about any reader of these words.

What we do not have are entire categories of information – Shakespeare's private letters or diaries, drafts and revisions of poems and plays, critical prefaces or essays, commendatory verse for other writers' works, or instructions guiding his fellow actors in their performances, for instance – that we imagine would help us understand and appreciate his surviving writings. For all we know, many such data never existed as written records. Many literary and theatrical critics, not knowing what might once have existed, more or less cheerfully accept the situation; some even make a theoretical virtue of it by claiming that such data are irrelevant to understanding and interpreting the plays and poems.

So, what do we know about William Shakespeare, the man responsible for thirty-seven or perhaps more plays, more than 150 sonnets, two lengthy narrative poems, and some shorter poems?

While many families by the name of Shakespeare (or some variant spelling) can be identified in the English Midlands as far back as the twelfth century, it seems likely that the dramatist's grandfather, Richard, moved to Snitterfield, a town not far from Stratford-upon-Avon, sometime before 1529. In Snitterfield, Richard Shakespeare leased farmland from the very wealthy Robert Arden. By 1552, Richard's son John had moved to a large house on Henley Street in Stratford-upon-Avon, the house that stands today as "The Birthplace." In Stratford, John Shakespeare traded as a glover, dealt in wool, and lent money at interest; he also served in a variety of civic posts, including "High Bailiff," the municipality's equivalent of mayor. In 1557, he married Robert Arden's youngest daughter, Mary. Mary and John had four sons – William was the oldest – and four daughters, of whom only Joan outlived her most celebrated sibling. William was baptized (an event entered in the Stratford parish church records) on April 26, 1564, and it has become customary, without any good factual support, to suppose he was born on April 23, which happens to be the feast day of Saint George, patron saint of England, and is also the date on which he died, in 1616. Shakespeare married Anne Hathaway in 1582, when he was eighteen and she was twenty-six; their first child was born five months later. It has been generally assumed that the marriage was enforced and subsequently unhappy, but these are only assumptions; it has been estimated, for instance, that up to one third of Elizabethan brides were pregnant when they married. Anne and William Shakespeare had three children: Susanna, who married a prominent local physician, John Hall; and the twins Hamnet, who died young in 1596, and Judith, who married Thomas Quiney – apparently a rather shady individual. The name Hamnet was unusual but not unique: he and his twin sister were named for their godparents, Shakespeare's neighbors Hamnet and Judith Sadler. Shakespeare's father died in 1601 (the year of *Hamlet*), and Mary Arden Shakespeare died in 1608 (the year of *Coriolanus*). William Shakespeare's last surviving direct descendant was his granddaughter Elizabeth Hall, who died in 1670.

Between the birth of the twins in 1585 and a clear reference to Shakespeare as a practicing London dramatist in Robert Greene's sensationalizing, satiric pamphlet, *Greene's Groatsworth of Wit* (1592), there is no record of where William Shakespeare was or what he was doing. These seven so-called lost years have been imaginatively filled by scholars and other students of Shakespeare: some think he traveled to Italy, or fought in the Low Countries, or studied law or medicine, or worked as an apprentice actor/writer, and so on to even more fanciful possibilities. Whatever the biographical facts for those "lost" years, Greene's nasty remarks in 1592 testify to professional envy and to the fact that Shakespeare already had a successful career in London. Speaking to his fellow playwrights, Greene warns both generally and specifically:

> . . . trust them [actors] not: for there is an upstart crow, beautified with our feathers, that with his tiger's heart wrapped in a player's hide supposes he is as well able to bombast out a blank verse as the best of you; and being an absolute Johannes Factotum, is in his own conceit the only Shake-scene in a country.

The passage mimics a line from *3 Henry VI* (hence the play must have been performed before Greene wrote) and seems to say that "Shake-scene" is both actor and playwright, a jack-of-all-trades. That same year, Henry Chettle protested Greene's remarks in *Kind-Heart's Dream,* and each of the next two years saw the publication of poems — *Venus and Adonis* and *The Rape of Lucrece,* respectively — publicly ascribed to (and dedicated by) Shakespeare. Early in 1595 he was named as one of the senior members of a prominent acting company, the Lord Chamberlain's Men, when they received payment for court performances during the 1594 Christmas season.

Clearly, Shakespeare had achieved both success and reputation in London. In 1596, upon Shakespeare's application, the College of Arms granted his father the now-familiar coat of arms he had taken the first steps to obtain almost twenty years before, and in 1598, John's son – now permitted to call himself "gentleman" – took a 10 percent share in the new Globe playhouse. In 1597, he bought a substantial bourgeois house, called New Place, in Stratford – the garden remains, but Shakespeare's house, several times rebuilt, was torn down in 1759 – and over the next few years Shakespeare spent large sums buying land and making other investments in the town and its environs. Though he worked in London, his family remained in Stratford, and he seems always to have considered Stratford the home he would eventually return to. Something approaching a disinterested appreciation of Shakespeare's popular and professional status appears in Francis Meres's *Palladis Tamia* (1598), a not especially imaginative and perhaps therefore persuasive record of literary reputations. Reviewing contemporary English writers, Meres lists the titles of many of Shakespeare's plays, including one not now known, *Love's Labor's Won,* and praises his "mellifluous & hony-tongued" "sugred Sonnets," which were then circulating in manuscript (they were first collected in 1609). Meres describes Shakespeare as "one of the best" English playwrights of both comedy and tragedy. In *Remains . . . Concerning Britain* (1605), William Camden – a more authoritative source than the imitative Meres – calls Shakespeare one of the "most pregnant witts of these our times" and joins him with such writers as Chapman, Daniel, Jonson, Marston, and Spenser. During the first decades of the seventeenth century, publishers began to attribute numerous play quartos, including some non-Shakespearean ones, to Shakespeare, either by name or initials, and we may assume that they deemed Shakespeare's name and supposed authorship, true or false, commercially attractive.

For the next ten years or so, various records show

Shakespeare's dual career as playwright and man of the theater in London, and as an important local figure in Stratford. In 1608-9 his acting company – designated the "King's Men" soon after King James had succeeded Queen Elizabeth in 1603 – rented, refurbished, and opened a small interior playing space, the Blackfriars theater, in London, and Shakespeare was once again listed as a substantial sharer in the group of proprietors of the playhouse. By May 11, 1612, however, he describes himself as a Stratford resident in a London lawsuit – an indication that he had withdrawn from day-to-day professional activity and returned to the town where he had always had his main financial interests. When Shakespeare bought a substantial residential building in London, the Blackfriars Gatehouse, close to the theater of the same name, on March 10, 1613, he is recorded as William Shakespeare "of Stratford upon Avon in the county of Warwick, gentleman," and he named several London residents as the building's trustees. Still, he continued to participate in theatrical activity: when the new Earl of Rutland needed an allegorical design to bear as a shield, or *impresa,* at the celebration of King James's Accession Day, March 24, 1613, the earl's accountant recorded a payment of 44 shillings to Shakespeare for the device with its motto.

For the last few years of his life, Shakespeare evidently concentrated his activities in the town of his birth. Most of the final records concern business transactions in Stratford, ending with the notation of his death on April 23, 1616, and burial in Holy Trinity Church, Stratford-upon-Avon.

THE QUESTION OF AUTHORSHIP

The history of ascribing Shakespeare's plays (the poems do not come up so often) to someone else began, as it continues, peculiarly. The earliest published claim that someone else wrote Shakespeare's plays appeared in an 1856 article by Delia Bacon in the American journal *Putnam's Monthly* – although an Englishman, Thomas Wilmot, had shared his doubts in private (even secretive) conversations with friends near the end of the eighteenth century. Bacon's was a sad personal history that ended in madness and poverty, but the year after her article, she published, with great difficulty and the bemused assistance of Nathaniel Hawthorne (then United States Consul in Liverpool, England), her *Philosophy of the Plays of Shakspere Unfolded*. This huge, ornately written, confusing farrago is almost unreadable; sometimes its intents, to say nothing of its arguments, disappear entirely beneath near-raving, ecstatic writing. Tumbled in with much supposed "philosophy" appear the claims that Francis Bacon (from whom Delia Bacon eventually claimed descent), Walter Ralegh, and several other contemporaries of Shakespeare's had written the plays. The book had little impact except as a ridiculed curiosity.

Once proposed, however, the issue gained momentum among people whose conviction was the greater in proportion to their ignorance of sixteenth- and seventeenth-century English literature, history, and society. Another American amateur, Catherine P. Ashmead Windle, made the next influential contribution to the cause when she published *Report to the British Museum* (1882), wherein she promised to open "the Cipher of Francis Bacon," though what she mostly offers, in the words of S. Schoenbaum, is "demented allegorizing." An entire new cottage industry grew from Windle's suggestion that the texts contain hidden, cryptographically discoverable ciphers – "clues" – to their authorship; and today there are not only books devoted to the putative ciphers, but also pamphlets, journals, and newsletters.

Although Baconians have led the pack of those seeking a substitute Shakespeare, in *"Shakespeare" Identified* (1920), J. Thomas Looney became the first published

"Oxfordian" when he proposed Edward de Vere, seventeenth earl of Oxford, as the secret author of Shakespeare's plays. Also for Oxford and his "authorship" there are today dedicated societies, articles, journals, and books. Less popular candidates – Queen Elizabeth and Christopher Marlowe among them – have had adherents, but the movement seems to have divided into two main contending factions, Baconian and Oxfordian. (For further details on all the candidates for "Shakespeare," see S. Schoenbaum, *Shakespeare's Lives,* 2nd ed., 1991.)

The Baconians, the Oxfordians, and supporters of other candidates have one trait in common – they are snobs. Every pro-Bacon or pro-Oxford tract sooner or later claims that the historical William Shakespeare of Stratford-upon-Avon could not have written the plays because he could not have had the training, the university education, the experience, and indeed the imagination or background their author supposedly possessed. Only a learned genius like Bacon or an aristocrat like Oxford could have written such fine plays. (As it happens, lucky male children of the middle class had access to better education than most aristocrats in Elizabethan England – and Oxford was not particularly well educated.) Shakespeare received in the Stratford grammar school a formal education that would daunt many college graduates today; and popular rival playwrights such as the very learned Ben Jonson and George Chapman, both of whom also lacked university training, achieved great artistic success, without being taken as Bacon or Oxford.

Besides snobbery, one other quality characterizes the authorship controversy: lack of evidence. A great deal of testimony from Shakespeare's time shows that Shakespeare wrote Shakespeare's plays and that his contemporaries recognized them as distinctive and distinctly superior. (Some of that contemporary evidence is collected in E. K. Chambers, *William Shakespeare: A Study of Facts and Problems,* 2 vols., 1930.) Since that testimony comes from Shakespeare's enemies and theatrical competitors as well as from his co-workers and from the Elizabethan equivalent of literary journalists, it seems unlikely that, if any of these sources had known he was a fraud, they would have failed to record that fact.

Books About Shakespeare's Theater

Useful scholarly studies of theatrical life in Shakespeare's day include: G. E. Bentley, *The Jacobean and Caroline Stage,* 7 vols. (1941-68), and the same author's *The Professions of Dramatist and Player in Shakespeare's Time, 1590-1642* (1986); E. K. Chambers, *The Elizabethan Stage,* 4 vols. (1923); R. A. Foakes, *Illustrations of the English Stage, 1580-1642* (1985); Andrew Gurr, *The Shakespearean Stage,* 3rd ed. (1992), and the same author's *Play-going in Shakespeare's London,* 2nd ed. (1996); Edwin Nungezer, *A Dictionary of Actors* (1929); Carol Chillington Rutter, ed., *Documents of the Rose Playhouse* (1984).

Books About Shakespeare's Life

The following books provide scholarly, documented accounts of Shakespeare's life: G. E. Bentley, *Shakespeare: A Biographical Handbook* (1961); E. K. Chambers, *William Shakespeare: A Study of Facts and Problems,* 2 vols. (1930); S. Schoenbaum, *William Shakespeare: A Compact Documentary Life* (1977); and *Shakespeare's Lives,* 2nd ed. (1991), by the same author. Many scholarly editions of Shakespeare's complete works print brief compilations of essential dates and events. References to Shakespeare's works up to 1700 are collected in C. M. Ingleby et al., *The Shakespeare Allusion-Book,* rev. ed., 2 vols. (1932).

The Texts of Shakespeare

As far as we know, only one manuscript conceivably in Shakespeare's own hand may (and even this is much disputed) exist: a few pages of a play called *Sir Thomas More*, which apparently was never performed. What we do have, as later readers, performers, scholars, students, are printed texts. The earliest of these survive in two forms: quartos and folios. Quartos (from the Latin for "four") are small books, printed on sheets of paper that were then folded in fours, to make eight double-sided pages. When these were bound together, the result was a squarish, eminently portable volume that sold for the relatively small sum of sixpence (translating in modern terms to about $5.00). In folios, on the other hand, the sheets are folded only once, in half, producing large, impressive volumes taller than they are wide. This was the format for important works of philosophy, science, theology, and literature (the major precedent for a folio Shakespeare was Ben Jonson's *Works*, 1616). The decision to print the works of a popular playwright in folio is an indication of how far up on the social scale the theatrical profession had come during Shakespeare's lifetime. The Shakespeare folio was an expensive book, selling for between fifteen and eighteen shillings, depending on the binding (in modern terms, from about $150 to $180). Twenty Shakespeare plays of the thirty-seven that survive first appeared in quarto, seventeen of which appeared during Shakespeare's lifetime; the rest of the plays are found only in folio.

The First Folio was published in 1623, seven years after Shakespeare's death, and was authorized by his fellow actors, the co-owners of the King's Men. This publication was certainly a mark of the company's enormous respect for Shakespeare; but it was also a way of turning the old plays, most of which were no longer current in the playhouse, into ready money (the folio includes only Shakespeare's plays, not his sonnets or other nondramatic verse). Whatever the motives behind the publication of the folio, the texts it preserves constitute the basis for almost all later editions of the playwright's works. The texts, however, differ from those of the earlier quartos, sometimes in minor respects but often significantly – most strikingly in the two texts of *King Lear,* but also in important ways in *Hamlet, Othello,* and *Troilus and Cressida.* (The variants are recorded in the textual notes to each play in the new Pelican series.) The differences in these texts represent, in a sense, the essence of theater: the texts of plays were initially not intended for publication. They were scripts, designed for the actors to perform – the principal life of the play at this period was in performance. And it follows that in Shakespeare's theater the playwright typically had no say either in how his play was performed or in the disposition of his text – he was an employee of the company. The authoritative figures in the theatrical enterprise were the shareholders in the company, who were for the most part the major actors. They decided what plays were to be done; they hired the playwright and often gave him an outline of the play they wanted him to write. Often, too, the play was a collaboration: the company would retain a group of writers, and parcel out the scenes among them. The resulting script was then the property of the company, and the actors would revise it as they saw fit during the course of putting it on stage. The resulting text belonged to the company. The playwright had no rights in it once he had been paid. (This system survives largely intact in the movie industry, and most of the playwrights of Shakespeare's time were as anonymous as most screenwriters are today.) The script could also, of course, continue to change as the tastes of audiences and the requirements of the actors changed. Many – perhaps most – plays were revised when they were reintroduced after any substantial absence from the repertory, or when they were performed by a company different from the one that originally commissioned the play.

Shakespeare was an exceptional figure in this world because he was not only a shareholder and actor in his company, but also its leading playwright – he was literally his own boss. He had, moreover, little interest in the publication of his plays, and even those that appeared during his lifetime with the authorization of the company show no signs of any editorial concern on the part of the author. Theater was, for Shakespeare, a fluid and supremely responsive medium – the very opposite of the great classic canonical text that has embodied his works since 1623.

The very fluidity of the original texts, however, has meant that Shakespeare has always had to be edited. Here is an example of how problematic the editorial project inevitably is, a passage from the most famous speech in *Romeo and Juliet,* Juliet's balcony soliloquy beginning "O Romeo, Romeo, wherefore art thou Romeo?" Since the eighteenth century, the standard modern text has read,

> What's Montague? It is nor hand, nor foot,
> Nor arm, nor face, nor any other part
> Belonging to a man. O be some other name!
> What's in a name? That which we call a rose
> By any other name would smell as sweet.
>
> (II.2.40–44)

Editors have three early texts of this play to work from, two quarto texts and the folio. Here is how the First Quarto (1597) reads:

> Whats *Mountague?* It is nor hand nor foote,
> Nor arme, nor face, nor any other part.
> Whats in a name? That which we call a Rose,
> By any other name would smell as sweet:

Here is the Second Quarto (1599):

> Whats *Mountague ?* it is nor hand nor foote,
> Nor arme nor face, ô be some other name
> Belonging to a man.
> Whats in a name that which we call a rose,
> By any other word would smell as sweete,

And here is the First Folio (1623):

> What's *Mountague ?* it is nor hand nor foote,
> Nor arme, nor face, O be some other name
> Belonging to a man.
> What ? in a names that which we call a Rose,
> By any other word would smell as sweete,

There is in fact no early text that reads as our modern text does – and this is the most famous speech in the play. Instead, we have three quite different texts, all of which are clearly some version of the same speech, but none of which seems to us a final or satisfactory version. The transcendently beautiful passage in modern editions is an editorial invention: editors have succeeded in conflating and revising the three versions into something we recognize as great poetry. Is this what Shakespeare "really" wrote? Who can say? What we can say is that Shakespeare always had performance, not a book, in mind.

Books About the Shakespeare Texts

The standard study of the printing history of the First Folio is W. W. Greg, *The Shakespeare First Folio* (1955). J. K. Walton, *The Quarto Copy for the First Folio of Shakespeare* (1971), is a useful survey of the relation of the quartos to the folio. The second edition of Charlton Hinman's *Norton Facsimile* of the First Folio (1996), with a new introduction by Peter Blayney, is indispensable. Stanley Wells, Gary Taylor, John Jowett, and William Montgmery, *William Shakespeare: A Textual Companion,* keyed to the Oxford text, gives a comprehensive survey of the editorial situation for all the plays and poems.

THE GENERAL EDITORS

Introduction

THEATER COMPANIES that find themselves in financial trouble often announce a production of *A Midsummer Night's Dream* as a way to repair their sagging fortunes. It invariably sells tickets, and whether performed in a high-school Cafetorium or at the Royal Shakespeare Theatre in Stratford-upon-Avon, the play rarely fails to please the audience. Its predictable success owes something to the sure-fire last act, where the bad acting and excruciating verse of the play-within-the-play send people out of the theater in a jolly mood. A play in which inept amateurs perform a bad play is nearly indestructible, even when played by amateurs, and the ridiculous performance of "The most lamentable comedy and most cruel death of Pyramus and Thisby" is merely the ultimate delight in a constantly rewarding two hours in the theater. Shakespeare gives us what we want when we go to a comedy: foolishness, the triumph of love and youth, magic, poetry, laughter. But he also provides something we may not know we want, effects and meanings that distinguish the greatest comedy: these include an ironic awareness that the joys attained are necessarily costly, anxiety about the evanescence of the theatrical fantasy, and recognition that the world to which we must return is not so pretty. It is this combination of mirth and depth that makes *A Midsummer Night's Dream* one of Shakespeare's most enduring and meaningful comedies.

Through four centuries and different cultural phases the play has maintained its appeal and proved hospitable to a wide range of production styles. Some scholars believe that it was written for, or at least performed to celebrate, an aristocratic wedding at which Queen Elizabeth herself was a guest, and that perhaps the children of the wedding party were enlisted to play fairies; these conjectures remain plausible and attractive but unproved. The indefatigable London diarist Samuel Pepys saw the play in the 1660s and declared it "the most insipid ridiculous play that ever I saw in my life," but his condescension must have been an atypical response, for the comedy continued to hold the stage throughout the Restoration and the eighteenth century. Victorian and early-twentieth-century directors amplified the spectacle, giving Titania throngs of fairies swathed in tulle, engaging orchestras to perform Mendelssohn's incidental music (op. 61) to the play, and dressing the stage as realistically as possible with moonlight, thickets of greenery, and live bunnies. Rejecting such romantic extravagance, Peter Brook at Stratford in 1970 staged one of the most revolutionary and celebrated productions of this or any Shakespearean play: taking his cue from Theseus's comment that drama depends upon the imaginative cooperation of the audience, Brook stripped the stage of scenery, placed his actors in tie-dyed T-shirts before a stark white background, and allowed his Oberon and Puck to supervise the mortals from a pair of trapezes. In 1992 the Canadian director Robert Lepage, working at the National Theatre in London, reversed the pictorial style prized by his Victorian predecessors and sent his lovers into a forest so dismal and muddy that the management was obliged to issue slickers to customers seated in the first three rows. In addition to its numerous stage productions, the text has generated a host of films and adaptations and takeoffs, from Max Reinhardt's 1935 Hollywood version (with James Cagney as Bottom and Mickey Rooney as Puck), to Kenneth McMillan's ballet (using Mendelssohn's music), to Benjamin Britten's opera, to Woody Allen's *A Midsummer Night's Sex Comedy*. The abundance and success of these various adaptations, high and low, attest to the innate theatricality of the original. People who like the theater like *A Midsummer Night's Dream* at least in part because it is an act of Shakespearean self-justification — an imaginative defense of the imaginative faculty, a fantastic study of the power of fantasy, a theatrical work that asserts the value of the theater while also acknowledging its fakery and ephemerality.

Ambivalence about his own profession is merely one proof of Shakespeare's growing sensitivity to the complexities of the world he was representing on the stage. Written circa 1595, about five years into his career as a playwright, *A Midsummer Night's Dream* marks the beginning of his artistic maturity, and a reliable sign of that development is his insistence on scrutinizing everything – each event, character, word, idea – from several sides. He prompts the audience to such perspectival inquiry by developing a complex structure of parallel stories, complementary characters, and thematic oppositions. The Athenian court, where the action begins, is associated with the law, with reason, with civilization, property, parents, daylight. The wood outside Athens, to which the action moves, is the realm of magic, of sexuality, liberty, lovers, dreams, night. Theseus and Hippolyta preside over the mortal world, Oberon and Titania over the fairy kingdom, and each couple may be seen as a mirror image of the other, one decorous and reasonable, the other passionate and volatile. Since they never appear onstage at the same time, the two pairs are often portrayed by the same actors, a doubling that implies the interdependence of logic and sensuality. Shakespeare contrasts the young lovers in a different way. Helena and Hermia are physical opposites, the one tall and fair – the Elizabethan ideal of beauty ironically embodied in the rejected Helena – the other short and dark. He also upends the misogynist cliché of female inconstancy. Both young women remain faithful to their initial lovers, even though Lysander and Demetrius seem indistinguishable; here it is the men who transfer their affections, Demetrius once and Lysander twice. Day and night, male and female, law and liberty, reason and imagination, scorn and sympathy – all these antitheses make up a kinetic and compelling imaginary world. Shakespeare prompts the spectator to wonder at and reevaluate the complexity of human affection, to shift allegiance emotionally and intellectually, and ultimately to recognize the contribution of dissonance to the creation of harmony.

This complex music of ideas is immediately audible in the linguistic multiplicity of the text. *A Midsummer Night's Dream* is distinguished by its rich poetic texture, especially the intensity and appeal of its lyrical utterances. Some of these passionate moments must result from the same lyric impulse that produced *Romeo and Juliet,* a play written at about the same time, and they signify a noticeable expansion of Shakespeare's poetic range. Titania's great elegy for the mother of the Indian boy (II.1.123-37), for example, displays a command of blank verse not found in the comedies written before this time, particularly in its use of sensuous imagery and rhythmic suppleness to create a melancholic tone. Almost half the play is written in rhyme – this is the highest proportion in the canon – and while some of these couplets clang ironically in the lamentations of Pyramus and Thisby, Shakespeare employs rhyme seriously as well. When attached to short iambic lines, rhyme identifies the sprightly voice of Puck: "Shall we their fond pageant see? / Lord, what fools these mortals be!" (III.2.114-15). Rhyme can also create the tones of incantation, as in the spell Oberon casts on his sleeping queen: "What thou seest when thou dost wake, / Do it for thy true love take" (II.2.27-28). Even more original is the poet's use of echo to intensify the sonorities of a serious passage: he rhymes long, unbroken lines of iambic pentameter and supplements the terminal harmonies with other aural effects, evoking a sense of mystery and resonant beauty. This tactic is clearly audible in Oberon's description of the "bank where the wild thyme blows, / Where oxlips and the nodding violet grows" (II.1.249-50). In brilliant contrast to the "wild thyme" speech is Titania's imperious declaration of love for Bottom: although her speech is composed in exactly the same form, rhymed iambic pentameter, its serious impact is subverted not only by the short declarative sentences but especially by the theatrical context – the fairy queen spends her eloquence upon an asinine weaver. Such opposing tones signify the young poet's realization of the multiple functions of music and poetry.

Shakespeare precisely calibrates the kinds of verse he creates for different characters and dramatic moments. Although he had successfully mixed poetry and prose in his earlier comedies, deploying each form for particular dramatic purposes, in *A Midsummer Night's Dream,* as the contrast between the two previous passages indicates, he achieves even greater affective precision. Another sign of this gift is the radical shift of registers to alter the dramatic tone. The fracas among the four lovers in Act Three, in which Demetrius and Lysander woo the incredulous Helena while insulting Hermia, is spoken mostly in iambic pentameter couplets, but at a crucial moment Helena shifts into blank verse to deliver her nostalgic plea for friendly sympathy:

> We, Hermia, like two artificial gods,
> Have with our needles created both one flower,
> Both on one sampler, sitting on one cushion,
> Both warbling of one song, both in one key;
> As if our hands, our sides, voices, and minds
> Had been incorporate. So we grew together,
> Like to a double cherry, seeming parted,
> But yet an union in partition,
> Two lovely berries molded on one stem.
>
> (III.2.203-11)

This and other lyrics coexist with pentameter couplets, with the reasonable blank verse measures of the Athenian court, with jigging pairs and triplets of rhyming tetrameter, with fairy songs, and with the thumping verse of the play-within-the-play:

> But stay: O spite!
> But mark, poor knight,

> What dreadful dole is here?
>> Eyes, do you see?
>> How can it be?
> O dainty duck, O dear!
>>> (V.1.271–76)

Finally, almost twenty percent of the text of *A Midsummer Night's Dream* is in prose, spoken mostly by the "mechanicals," and even in this medium Shakespeare produces aural effects seldom heard in English comedy to this point. The craftsmen plan their festival play and conduct the rehearsal in workmanlike, everyday prose, much of it studded with malapropisms and other blunders. And yet the poet employs the same simple materials to create, in the soliloquy in which Bottom recalls his night in the forest, one of the most delicate moments in all of Shakespearean comedy, a parody of a religious epiphany that manages to evoke the emotional potency of the real thing.

The poetic range – from lyrical to ludicrous – corresponds to and helps to produce the tonal diversity that makes the play so appealing. Most comedy moves toward an affirmative resolution, the happy ending that emphasizes reconciliation and the satisfaction of desire. Audiences rejoice emotionally in the marriage of young people with whom they have identified and sympathized. At the same time, however, most comedy diverts its audience with preposterous behavior, developing conflicts that imply separation, error, reversal, and frustration. Even as we anticipate a happy ending, we take pleasure in watching shenanigans, pretension, and the well-aimed custard pie. This tension amounts to a contest between the end and the middle: the resolution provokes laughter of satisfaction; the comic conflict, laughter of scorn. Looked at from another angle, this opposition may be regarded as a struggle between the claims of irony and romance. In *The Defence of Poesy*, written about 1580, Sir Philip Sidney applauded the representation of foolish behavior, asserting that comedy fulfilled the moral function of leading audiences to reject such action with dismissive laughter. Practicing playwrights, however, like their modern counterparts, knew that audiences liked to leave the theater feeling hopeful, comforted by the belief that obstacles could be surmounted and happiness achieved. Comic fiction almost always cultivates both kinds of response. Jane Austen, for example, rewards the reader of *Pride and Prejudice* with both the idiocy of Mr. Collins and Mrs. Bennet and the reciprocated affections of Elizabeth and Darcy.

A Midsummer Night's Dream has proved hospitable to so many different styles of production because it makes available to the director and the audience an exceptionally broad range of potential response. The ending offers multiple satisfactions: three human marriages are celebrated in the final scene, the fairy king and queen are reconciled, Bottom and the mechanicals believe that their court performance is a triumph, and as the lovers go off to bed, the fairies enter the palace to bless the marriages. And yet the concord and the delight generated by the conclusion are counterbalanced not only by the embarrassing antics that the characters have displayed on the way to the final scene, but also by the playwright's stimulation of doubt about whether joy at the happy ending is actually warranted. Shakespeare seems to challenge any easy and uncritical pleasure in the marriage of the four young people, the union of Theseus and Hippolyta, the reconciliation of the supernatural figures, and, most obviously, the achievement of the amateur thespians. What looks like a joyous romp turns out to have darker reaches. This disturbance beneath the surface becomes one of Shakespeare's major themes in *A Midsummer Night's Dream* as the audience discovers that everything is more complicated than it first appears, a principle that applies most significantly to the theater itself.

It is not surprising that a play so self-conscious about the nature and value of fiction should display as many different literary influences as this one. Shakespeare remembered Chaucer's Knight's Tale for the story of Theseus and Hippolyta; he must have known the mythic comedies written for Elizabeth's court by John Lyly during the previous decade; and he appropriated the appeals of such popular romances as Apuleius's *The Golden Ass* and the French *Huon of Bordeaux*. The text contains allusions to the Bible and more indirect echoes of humanist versions of some major Platonic texts. But the most potent of all literary influences is Ovid's *Metamorphoses*, the collection of fabulous stories written by the Roman poet and translated into English by Arthur Golding in the 1560s. Its fantastic tales of transformation – of Actaeon changed into a stag and devoured by his hounds, of Galatea changed from statue to living woman – find their way into Shakespeare's work from the beginning of his career to the end, but nowhere is their influence more telling than in *A Midsummer Night's Dream*. His attraction to these legendary tales of mysterious change is obvious in the narrative turns that shape the comedy: Oberon's scheme against his recalcitrant queen, the alteration of the young Athenians' affections, above all the transformation of Bottom. An even greater stimulus to Shakespeare, however, was Ovid's imaginative expansion of what is normally taken to be "reality," his creation of a realm in which nature is subject to, and should be seen as the physical manifestation of, some indefinable and providential artistry.

The extraordinary scope of *A Midsummer Night's Dream* is not only poetic and tonal: its characters range from the world of the lower-class craftsmen, the "rude mechanicals," through the courtly world of the mortal lovers, to the supernatural sphere of Oberon and Titania, King and Queen of the Fairies. Shakespeare's enthusiasm for Ovid probably accounts for his representation of the spirit world, the feature that gives *A Midsummer Night's Dream* its magical flavor and sets it apart from most of his other comedies. Although supernatural events and beings appear in many different kinds of drama – the god who

arrives to bless the marriages in *As You Like It,* the aveng-
ing spirits in *Richard III,* Banquo's ghost in *Macbeth,* the
magic in the last plays – in most of the comedies Shakespeare confines himself to the material world. This is not
to say, of course, that the action of any of his comedies is
"realistic": an urban farce like *The Comedy of Errors* is as
much a fantasy as *A Midsummer Night's Dream.* But the
supernatural is intrinsic to the meaning of *Dream.* In the
first place, the fairy king and queen embody the forces
that comic writers use – such forces are normally unseen – to imply providential protection of their human
characters. Shakespeare's practice here is hardly simple:
Oberon, quarrelsome, dependent on fallible agents, and
prone to error and jealousy, is not precisely the equivalent
of God. But he acts as deus ex machina, his ministrations
bringing about the happy ending for the mortals. What is
even more significant is that the fairy kingdom serves the
playwright as a means of depicting and investigating
the mysterious workings of the human imagination. At
the risk of oversimplifying a symbolic relation explored
with great subtlety, we may say that the fairy kingdom is
to the natural world as the unconscious is to the conscious
mind, or the imaginative to the logical faculty. This corre-
spondence is thematically crucial, the relation to which all
the other parallels and contrasts between the human and
the fairy world contribute.

The everyday world is profoundly affected by the supernatural realm, as the audience discovers when the
scene changes from Athens to the wood, at the beginning
of Act Two. Puck's description of his role as Oberon's
jester (II.1.43–58) attributes those human accidents and
errors that defy logical explanation to the trickery of the
spirit world, and the quarrel between Titania and Oberon
immediately following this recital clarifies and reinforces
this supernatural determination of mortal affairs. In her
outburst to Oberon, "These are the forgeries of jealousy,"
the fairy queen laments that their vengeful dispute should
have disrupted the seasons and produced miserable

weather in the human world. Magical intervention also accounts for those twists that the lovers attribute to logic: their efforts to rationalize their changing affections ironically expose the inadequacy of reason to explain much human perplexity. Awakening from slumber, Lysander declares and justifies his newfound passion for Helena in just these terms: "The will of man is by his reason swayed, / And reason says you are the worthier maid" (II.2.115–16). But reason has nothing to do with it: the audience has just watched Puck anoint Lysander's eyes with juice from the love-in-idleness flower. Given Puck's pleasure in his responsibility for human error, it is worth observing that his application of the liquid to Lysander's eyelids is itself a mistake, a bungled attempt to follow Oberon's orders about transforming the young Athenian so that he will yield to Helena. Puck gets the wrong fellow. A thoughtful audience might be led to wonder about the source of Puck's blunder.

Reason is an especially faulty guide in matters of affection. In the middle of the comedy, the queen of fairies awakens under the influence of a magical spell to find herself irresistibly attracted to the grotesque Bottom, who has himself been supernaturally transformed into an ass. His reaction to Titania's passionate expression of love is skeptical: "Methinks, mistress, you should have little reason for that. And yet, to say the truth, reason and love keep little company together nowadays" (III.1.136–38). The hilarity of the moment should not obscure the Shakespearean home truth that Bottom enunciates: the incompatibility of head and heart. The supremacy of "cool reason," to which Theseus subscribes absolutely and uncritically, is subverted most thoroughly in his famous attack on fantasy (V.1.2–22), where he smugly lumps together the lunatic, the lover, and the poet, and mocks belief in "fairy toys" or supernatural fables. Shakespeare pointedly challenges Theseus's rational position with a host of situational ironies. In the first place, the audience has witnessed the supernatural machinations that have altered the desires of Lysander, Demetrius, and Titania. Moreover, Theseus himself is a lover who articulates his distrust of the imagination in a graceful, poetic speech. He is, in other words, a product of Shakespeare's imagination, and the audience can hardly miss these contradictions. Hippolyta, on the other hand, intuits the truth of what the lovers have reported about their transformation:

> But all the story of the night told over,
> And all their minds transfigured so together,
> More witnesseth than fancy's images
> And grows to something of great constancy.
> (V.1.23-26)

Our awareness of the story of the night confirms her suspicion and mocks Theseus's self-assurance: Shakespeare has given us evidence of things not seen.

Throughout *A Midsummer Night's Dream* the metaphysical or the supernatural is associated with eros because, as always in Shakespeare, amorous desire is inexplicable, irrational. It remains oblivious to parental pressure, legal edict, even cruel rejection by the beloved, and desire will ultimately have its way. In almost all the comedies the young woman is rewarded with the young man she wants despite mighty obstacles – e.g., Rosalind in *As You Like It,* Viola in *Twelfth Night,* and Portia in *The Merchant of Venice.* Even when the object of affection seems unworthy of the heroine – Proteus and Julia in *The Two Gentlemen of Verona* and Bertram and Helena in *All's Well That Ends Well* spring to mind – the audience endorses her desire and rejoices in her success. In *A Midsummer Night's Dream* Hermia loves Lysander, not Demetrius, and never wavers in her affection. Likewise, Helena irrationally dotes on Demetrius in spite of his scorn for her. Everybody in Athens knows that Helena is as good-looking as Hermia, but that fact makes no difference to Demetrius: "He *will* not know what all but he do know" (I.1.229). My emphasis of the word "will" – and I follow the dictates of the iambic construction – is intended to indicate the complexity of the emotion that goes by the name of "love." "Will" in the sixteenth century was not only a verbal statement of intention but also a synonym for sexual desire: as we know from Sonnets 135 and 136, in which Shakespeare puns on his first name, the word could also refer, depending on context, to the penis or vagina. Love in *A Midsummer Night's Dream* is compounded of physical attraction, imaginative sympathy ("Love looks not with the eyes, but with the mind," I.1.234), the wish to possess or control, and a kind of irrational obsession or "dotage." And love is immensely forceful, as Helena asserts in her pouty soliloquy at the end of the first scene: "Things base and vile, holding no quantity, / Love can transpose to form and dignity" (I.1.232-33). It exerts such power because it originates in that dynamic faculty that Shakespeare opposes to the workings of reason, the human imagination.

If Theseus's court is the domain of reason, the nocturnal forest is the home of the imagination. Shakespearean comedy often depends upon an opposition between the familiar, well-lighted world of the city or the court and the exotic freedom of the green world, a structural contrast most thoroughly developed in *As You Like It*. As people move from known to alien territory, dislocation fosters reevaluation and self-discovery. The forest to which the lovers retreat in *A Midsummer Night's Dream* is dark and potentially perilous, but it is ironically a site of revelation and recognition. The possibilities for illumination are captured in Demetrius's triple pun on his frustration and confusion in the forest: "Thou told'st me they were stol'n unto this wood, / And here am I, and wood within this wood / Because I cannot meet my Hermia" (II.1.191-93). Demetrius's inability to find Hermia in the forest drives him mad: "wood" means both "forest" and "insane," and he is being "wooed" by Helena. Wooing or courtship, the social form of sexual desire, propels the lovers into a state of madness, and the wood is Shakespeare's arena for exhibiting the irrational sources and effects of passion, the province of lunatics, lovers, and poets.

Theseus's ridicule of fantasy is the most direct assault on the imaginative faculty, but it is by no means the only one, and each of the doubters is mocked in turn. Peter Quince's craftsmen exhibit a materialist bias in their rehearsal for the duke's entertainment, fretting over how to present the formidable special effects required by their script, particularly the entrance of the lion and the effect of moonlight. In both cases they think literally, crediting the audience with no power to distinguish a stage lion from the real animal or to *suppose* that moonlight suffuses the dramatic scene. They forget, of course, that their prospective audience, like any set of spectators, has already taken an enormous mental leap in believing actors to be characters at all, especially in accepting a weaver and a bellows mender as legendary doomed lovers. Shakespeare, on the other hand, is acutely conscious of the potentiality of that imaginative commitment, and it is this reflexive concern with the audience's role in the making of fiction that prompts his subtle and searching consideration of imaginative possibility.

The audience apprehends Shakespeare's interest in the relation of desire and imagination through a series of semantically interconnected nouns. All the cardinal values of comedy – love, freedom, community, generation, play – derive from the activity of the imagination, and "imagination" is linked etymologically with two other roots reiterated throughout the play, "image" and "magic." When Helena identifies the origins of eros in mental images – "Love looks not with the eyes, but with the mind" – she identifies the psychological process that allows Oberon to alter the lovers' affections with the magical liquid and its antidote. Something magical happens, juice or no juice, in the lover's mind, which produces images of the beloved – "fancies" or "fantasies" – that are mediated by the eyes but proceed from the imagination. The lovesick Helena is said to be "fancy-sick." Although Theseus instructs Hermia, "fit your fancies to your father's will" (I.1.118) – that is, obey Egeus's commands – such fancies or fantasies cannot be altered or re-"fit"; they are mysterious, potent, and impervious to reasonable discourse. "Vision" is less important in its physical than in its metaphysical sense, the eye being mainly an aperture through which the imagination perceives the world and dictates to the heart. Thus, Oberon seeks revenge on Titania by using the magic essence to "streak her eyes / And make her full of hateful fantasies" (II.1.257-58). He takes pains to trace the liquid's derivation from love-in-idleness, the plant more commonly known as the pansy: the name originates in the French term *pensée,* for "thought" or "reflection." The flower is thus related to the imaginative faculty and its capacity to produce dreams, illusions, even madness ("wood within this wood"). Theseus's analysis of "strong imagination," that it "tricks" us into wild surmises and "bodies forth / The forms of things unknown" (V.1.14-15), is patronizing and dismissive, but it is much more accurate and meaningful than he recognizes, especially his identification of love and madness. "Image," "magic," "imagination," "fancy," "fantasy," "vision," "illusion," "play" – the languages of love and creativity are meaningfully interlaced.

The word "dream" in the title, along with the various dreams and visions that drive the action, attests to the revelatory possibilities of the unconscious. When Lysander magically shifts his attentions to Helena, his unwitting infidelity is figured in Hermia's nightmare (II.2.145-56), in which Lysander sits smiling as a serpent gnaws at Hermia's heart. Freudian credentials are not required to analyze such a nocturnal fantasy. When the dawn does arrive, the moment of awakening generates a variety of reactions to events of the night. Titania muses ruefully on her half-remembered experience: "My Oberon, what visions have I seen!" (IV.1.75). Her proper perception having been restored, she feels only disgust at the sleeping Bottom: "O, how mine eyes do loathe his *visage* now!" (l. 78; emphasis mine). The four lovers sense that something has changed but confess themselves unable to explain it. Demetrius, for example, relies on natural metaphors ("Melted as the snow," "as in health, come to my natural taste") to account for his altered feelings. Bottom is the last of the Athenians to discover the potent effects of dreams, and his fumbling meditation (IV.1.199–217) captures the mysterious interpenetration of the conscious and the unconscious. He knows that something momentous has occurred, but he knows that he would make an ass of himself if he tried to explain it. His impulse, however, is to give it permanence, to fix it so that it can be examined and admired, and to that end he will have Peter Quince convert his "dream" into a ballad to be sung at the end of the mechanicals' play. This wish once more connects the mysterious ways of the imagination with that theatrical product of the imagination in which Bottom is now performing and which the audience is watching: the word "illusion" derives from *lūdere,* Latin for "play." Plays functioned in sixteenth-century English culture as movies do in our own, as powerful visual fantasies. Stage action and characters constitute an alternative imaginative realm into which the spectators can project themselves. *A Midsummer Night's Dream* permits the audience to participate in the vicarious pleasures of a comic structure: the triumph of youth, the fulfillment of desire, the defeat of confusion and disappointment.

And yet the play barely suppresses a vigorous countermovement that must inevitably trouble the thoughtful spectator. The happy outcome cannot efface the error and embarrassment of which the triumphant characters have been guilty, and the most common of these weaknesses is pride. Oberon in his first speech berates his queen for her vanity, and their argument shortly reveals that hubris and its attendant faults are a root cause of their dispute and thus of its far-reaching consequences. Ostensibly they quarrel over possession of a child, the son of one of Titania's priestesses: she loves him as a reminder of his dead mother, while Oberon wants to take the boy from her and make him part of his retinue. But the contention seems to be less about possession of the Indian boy himself than about self-assertion and wounded pride. Oberon appears injured by Titania's neglect of him, by the threat to his primacy, while her attachment to the child may be construed as a form of willfulness and exclusion. Such tensions radiate into other regions of the action, most notably the decorous bickering between Theseus and Hippolyta on the morning of the hunt. When she recalls the baying of the "hounds of Sparta" on a hunting trip with Hercules, Theseus must assert the superiority of his dogs and boast about the harmony of their barking. The hunting dogs, like the Indian boy, are not really the issue. Pride sometimes takes improbable forms, such as the amour propre that leads Helena to revel in her role as unrequited lover. The brawl among the young Athenians that makes up the third act degenerates into a bout of physical insults ("thou painted maypole," "You bead, you acorn!") and name-calling: "Where art thou, proud Demetrius?"; "Thou runaway, thou coward, art thou fled?" And anyone who has ever acted will recognize the egotism of Bottom's wish to do all the parts in the mechanicals' play.

The numerous expressions of self-regard begin in the generational dispute that opens the play and are developed in the ensuing gender conflicts. Egeus's assertion of his right to dictate his daughter's choice of husband exposes his view of her as no more than his possession, an extension of himself and his will:

> true, he hath *my* love,
> And what is *mine my* love shall render him,
> And she is *mine,* and all *my right* of her
> I do *estate* unto Demetrius.
> (I.1.95-98; emphasis mine)

The diction of property and possession links his claim to the extremes of patriarchal privilege, but such mechanical repetition of his paternal right makes him into one of those mechanical figures that comic writers use to focus the scorn of their audiences. To survey the various hierarchies and classes represented in the play – Theseus's court, the realm of the fairies, the craftsmen-thespians – is to find that conventional authority fares poorly in Athens and its environs. Peter Quince's direction is repeatedly challenged by Bottom, Oberon's instructions to Puck are mistakenly executed, and Theseus's smug confidence in his understanding of the world and the role of reason is shown to be insupportable. As comedy often does, *A Midsummer Night's Dream* affords its females most of the audience's sympathy, its men most of the ridicule. We are urged to identify with and endorse the desires of the constant Helena and Hermia, and the intuitive and sympathetic Hippolyta. The men, by contrast, are far less attractive, as three disparate examples will suggest. The swaggering machismo that motivates Lysander and Demetrius in their nocturnal mud-wrestling is very broadly drawn. Less obvious, perhaps, is the sexual anxiety that Theseus evinces in his instructions to Hippolyta on how to cope with amateur dramatics. Take the intention for the deed, he says; appreciate the good will and don't worry about the performance. It is worth pointing out that this lesson is enunciated on his wedding night by an aging bridegroom who is about to go to bed with an Amazon.

The most disturbing case of masculine pride is the resolution of Oberon's plot against Titania. Not only is her adoration of Bottom humiliating, but she surrenders the Indian boy without apparent protest and finally seems not to resent Oberon's prank. Even if we conclude that Oberon has cuckolded himself in getting his way, rarely is a Shakespearean episode inflected with so little irony. This resolution may be seen, however, as a harsh but necessary means of settling a cosmic struggle, an appropriate if still troubling victory over Titania's obstinacy. The quarrel ends with a dance, always a Shakespearean symbol of

order and harmony, and that outcome implies that
Oberon may be not merely a bully but a justifiably frustrated husband seeking to correct his wife's "dotage." It
may, in other words, serve as a warning against our invariably taking the woman's part. The play questions the received structures of society, but it ultimately restores and
accepts them.

Shakespeare's comic assault on the proud and their
smug conceptions of order and truth contributes to his
larger challenge to conventional notions of ontology – to
our sense, in other words, of who we are and what constitutes reality. If Puck's proud narration of the havoc he creates in the mortal world – causing spills, knocking old
ladies off stools – troubles our sense of causality and
human control, his own mistake in anointing the wrong
Athenian's eyes might provoke further speculation. Perhaps yet another unseen agent causes Puck to err for the
amusement of a higher god? As the four lovers make their
way back to Athens, they acknowledge their inability to
distinguish reality and illusion, mountains and clouds,
waking and dreaming. (In Benjamin Britten's operatic
version, this crucial moment is captured in a mysteriously
beautiful quartet, "And I have found Demetrius like a
jewel.") Shakespeare's manipulation of perspective takes
its most revelatory form in the arrangement of the play-within-the-play. During the performance of "Pyramus
and Thisby," we may imagine the stage and the theater
and the world as a series of concentric circles. At the very
center are Bottom and Flute, playing tragic lovers. They
are watched by actors playing the courtly lovers, characters whose experience might have paralleled that of the
doomed Pyramus and Thisby but who fail to notice the
similarity. They, in turn, are watched by the theater audience, spectators who laugh smugly at the smugness of the
onstage audience. This set of symmetries implies that we
may be mistaken in thinking of ourselves as the final audience. Isn't it possible that we, too, are performing for
unseen spectators, that our delight in the foolishness of

what we see may itself be a brand of folly, and that the world we take to be real may be nothing more than a stage set for a divine audience?

Such doubts about the nature of the real are confirmed by the play's multiple endings. As the mechanicals wrap up their play, Theseus condescendingly announces the arrival of "fairy time" and sends the lovers off to bed with a closing couplet, thus signaling the end of the play. But the grand exit of the cast is followed by the entrance of Puck, who recites rhymed verses that seem to constitute a benediction. Then: *Enter King and Queen of Fairies, with all their train.* Their song and dance represent the final blessing of the house, and as they all sweep off the stage, Puck advances to address the audience directly, thus demolishing the boundary between stage and gallery. His epilogue, "If we shadows have offended," speaks directly to the ontological problem of what we have seen. Does "shadows" refer to fairies or to actors? Both meanings are current in the sixteenth century. Is the audience being addressed by "Puck" or by the performer who has just finished enacting Puck? We have consented, for the previous two hours, to accept the stage action as reality, shadow as substance. Can we be sure that the world we have agreed to think of as real is anything more than a platform constructed for heavenly mirth? Where does the stage end and the world begin?

For all the laughter and pleasure that *A Midsummer Night's Dream* generates, it also questions the validity and permanence of its affirmations. The human imagination produces as many nightmares as beguiling visions: or, in the words of the great Spanish painter Goya, "the sleep of reason brings forth monsters." As the fairies bless the offspring of the wedded couples, we may uneasily recall the Ovidian sequel to the marriage of Theseus and Hippolyta: their son was the doomed Hippolytus, lusted after by his stepmother and ultimately regarded as a figure for the destructive power of passion. Even the delights of theatrical illusion are suspect. As Meredith Skura has argued, the affection and indulgence with which Shakespeare depicts Bottom will turn to self-loathing in the tragedies, where the player merely struts and frets his hour upon the stage, where imagination is self-annihilating, and where the world is so dark that illusion is always deceptive and usually fatal.* In the comedies, however, the harmonies and rewards of theatrical art are still available, and that is why, at this very moment, it is likely that *A Midsummer Night's Dream* is now playing at a theater near you.

Russ McDonald
University of North Carolina at Greensboro

---

*Shakespeare the Actor and the Purposes of Playing (Chicago: University of Chicago Press, 1993), p. 114.

Note on the Text

A MIDSUMMER NIGHT'S DREAM first appeared in print in
1600, in a quarto published by Thomas Fisher (he registered the play on October 8 of that year) and probably
printed by Richard Bradock. The title page assures the
prospective purchaser that this is the version that "hath
been sundry times publicly acted by the Right Hon-
ourable the Lord Chamberlain his Servants." Scholarly
scrutiny of the First Quarto (Q1) reveals that it was almost certainly set from Shakespeare's "foul papers," a
manuscript copy of the play written in his hand. Stage directions are sketchy (e.g., *Enter the Clownes* substitutes for
the enumeration of entering characters), and speech prefixes are sometimes inconsistent (Puck's lines, for example, are sometimes assigned to "Robin" or "Rob" and
sometimes to "Puck," many of Titania's to "Quee" or
"Qu," for Queen). This kind of evidence attests to an
early state of textual realization: in other words, the composing playwright allows himself inconsistencies or short-
cuts that would (or might) be regularized or clarified at
the later stage of theatrical production. Q1 is thus a re-
vealing window onto Shakespeare's compositional practice. Instances of old-fashioned spelling (e.g., "prooue" for
"prove," "vneauen" for "uneven") resemble those found in
the surviving fragment of *The Book of Sir Thomas More,*
believed by many to be in Shakespeare's handwriting. Especially interesting is the mislineation of certain passages
of verse in Act Five, particularly a famous section in Theseus's speech about "the lunatic, the lover, and the poet."
John Dover Wilson believed that the confusion arose
from the compositor's difficulty in reading marginal addi-
tions inserted by Shakespeare himself, lines that represented his revision and expansion of his preliminary

version of the scene. It is possible that, in composing the play, Shakespeare became increasingly taken with the power of the imaginative faculty and that he augmented the original speech, which identified love and madness, with the additional lines about poetic creativity. Whatever the source of the mislined passages, later editors progressively adjusted them into proper iambic form, and those changes to Q1 have been followed in the present edition.

In 1619 the Second Quarto (Q2) appeared, although its title page falsely claims 1600 as the date of publication. It is one of several such deceptive reprints made for the publisher William Jaggard. Although it offers a few helpful corrections to Q1, its main value to the modern editor is that it was used as the copy text for the edition of *Dream* that appears in the First Folio, 1623 (F). In preparing the text for the folio, the editors obviously consulted a playhouse manuscript along with a copy of Q2. Whereas the two quartos are notably sparse with exits, F offers an amplified set of theatrical instructions. In the final scene, for example, as the mechanicals enter in their Pyramus and Thisby costumes, F contains the following stage direction: *Tawyer with a Trumpet before them.* (William Tawyer was a servant or employee of John Hemings, a member of the King's Men and one of the compilers of the folio texts.) Another notable feature of F is its division of the play into acts: Q1 has no act divisions and does not number the scenes. When F, at the end of Act III, prints *They sleepe all the Act,* the direction may indicate that the lovers sleep until Theseus awakens them at IV.1.137. However, it may direct them to remain asleep onstage during an interval (or "act") between Acts Three and Four. Such a reading would suggest that the manuscript used to supplement the quarto text dates from at least fourteen years after the initial performances, since the King's Men apparently did not employ intervals in performance before about 1609.

The one substantive difference between the two quartos (QQ) and F concerns the status of Egeus, Hermia's father, in Act Five. In Q1, Theseus consults his master of the revels, Philostrate, about selecting an after-dinner entertainment. In F, although the lines are the same, Egeus describes the theatrical candidates, and a few of Theseus's lines (the reading of the titles) are transferred to Lysander. It can be argued that, since in Q1 Egeus is not present in Act Five, the folio version offers a warmer, more inclusive ending, with father and daughter obviously reconciled. Readers interested in pursuing the implications of these changes should consult Stanley Wells, Gary Taylor, John Jowett, and William Montgomery, *Shakespeare: A Textual Companion* (Oxford: Oxford University Press, 1987), pp. 279-87; Barbara Hodgdon, "Gaining a Father: The Role of Egeus in the Quarto and the Folio," *Review of English Studies, NS* 37 (1986), pp. 534-52; and Peter Holland's Oxford edition of the play (1994), pp. 257-68.

The present edition follows Q1, accepting a few alterations from Q2 and F (and one from the Second Folio, F2). Recent textual scholarship has revised the notion of a single "authoritative" text, demonstrating that the different versions of several Shakespearean plays must have represented "authorized" versions; that some of the texts were clearly revised by Shakespeare himself; and that early theatrical changes, whether devised by the author or not, represent a more or less legitimate version of the play in question. In the case of *A Midsummer Night's Dream,* both Q1 and F seem to be records of versions that were performed with Shakespeare's approval. Forced to choose between them, I have preferred Q1 as an example of a text that was performed for at least the first five years or so after its composition. Whether or not Shakespeare cared about the printing of his plays, his own manuscript made its way into the printing house and thus represents *an,* if not *the,* early authorial version of the play.

In speech prefixes, stage directions, and dialogue, the character who assists Oberon is designated both "Robin Goodfellow" and "Puck." Some scholars have recently urged that usage be regularized, preferring the character's given name (Robin) to the generic name for a mischievous spirit (Puck). While acknowledging the appeal of this argument, I have retained the inconsistencies of Q1 on the grounds that they represent the earliest extant version of the text, and that they could derive from authorial thinking about the character: for the most part, the given name refers to the independent spirit, the generic to Oberon's impish servant.

Significant departures from Q1 are recorded below. Obvious errors, original spelling, and improper lineation of poetic passages have been silently corrected or modernized. When changes have been made, the new reading is given in italics; the original quarto version is given in roman. Readings taken from Q2, F, or F2 are indicated parenthetically. Most other emendations are those traditionally accepted by Shakespearean scholarship; in a very few cases, the source of the change is identified in the footnotes within the text.

I.1 4 *wanes* (Q2, F) waues (Q1) 10 *New-bent* Now bent (QQ, F) 19 **s.d.** *omitting "Helena"* (F) including "Helena" (QQ) 24 *Stand forth, Demetrius* printed as s.d. (QQ, F) 26 *Stand forth, Lysander* printed as s.d. (QQ, F) 27 *This hath* (F2) This man hath (QQ, F) 136 *low* loue (QQ, F) 139 *merit* else, it (QQ, F) 187 *Yours would* Your words (QQ, F) 216 *sweet* sweld (QQ, F) 219 *stranger companies* strange companions (QQ, F)
I.2 24 *rest. Yet* rest yet (QQ, F) 25–26 *split. / "The* split the (QQ, F) 26–33 *"The raging . . . foolish Fates."* printed as prose (QQ, F)
II.1 61 *Fairies* Fairy (QQ, F) 69 *steep* (Q2, F steepe) steppe (Q1) 79 *Aegles* Eagles (QQ, F) 101 *cheer* heere (QQ, F) 109 *thin* chinne (QQ, F) 158 *by the* (F) by (QQ) 190 *slay . . . slayeth* stay . . . stayeth (QQ, F) 201 *nor I* (F) not I (QQ)
II.2 9 *FIRST FAIRY* not in QQ, F 39 *Be it* (Q2, F) Bet it (Q1) 43 *good* (Q2, F) god (Q1) 47 *is* (Q2, F) it (Q1)
III.1 27–28 *yourselves* (F) your selfe (QQ) 52 *BOTTOM* (Q2, F Bot.) Cet. (Q1) 63 *and let* or let (QQ, F) 77 *BOTTOM [As Pyramus]* Pyra. 78 *Odorous, odorous* Odours, odorous (QQ) Odours, odours (F) 79 *BOTTOM [As Pyramus]* Py. 83 *PUCK* (F) Quin. (QQ) 84 *FLUTE* Thys. 88 *FLUTE [As Thisby]* Thys. 90 *bristly* brisky (QQ, F) 97 *FLUTE [As Thisby]* Thys. 98 *BOTTOM [As Pyramus]* Py. 156–57 *PEASEBLOSSOM . . . go* Fairies. Readie: and I, and I, and I. Where shall we goe? (QQ, F) 169–72 *PEASEBLOSSOM . . . Hail* 1. Fai. Haile mortall, haile. / 2. Fai. Haile. / 3. Fai. Haile. (QQ, F) 189 *you of* you (QQ, F)
III.2 19 *mimic* (F Mimmick) Minnick (Q1) Minnock (Q2) 80 *part I so*

part I (QQ, F)   85 *sleep* slippe (Q1) slip (Q2, F)   213 *first, like* first life (QQ, F)   220 *passionate* (F) not in (QQ)   237 *Ay, do. Persever I doe.* Perseuer (Q1) I, do, perseuer (Q2, F)   250 *prayers* praise (QQ, F)   257 *No, no, sir, yield* No, no: heele (Q1) No, no, hee'l (Q2) No, no, Sir (F)   299 *gentlemen* (Q2, F) gentleman (Q1)   406 *Speak! In some bush?* Speake in some bush. (QQ, F)   451 *To your* your (QQ, F)

IV.1 23 *Peaseblossom* Cobwebbe (QQ, F)   41 *woodbine . . . honeysuckle* woodbine, . . . Honisuckle, (QQ, F)   65 *That, he* That hee, (Q1) That he (Q2, F)   72 *o'er* or (QQ, F)   81 *sleep of all these five* sleepe: of all these, fine (QQ, F)   116 *Seemed* Seeme (QQ, F)   127 *this is* (Q2, F) this (Q1)   132 *rite* right (QQ, F)   171 *saw* see (QQ, F)   198 *let us* (Q2, F) lets (Q1)   205 *to expound* (Q2, F) expound (Q1)   208 *a patched* (F) patcht a (QQ)   215 *our play* a Play (QQ, F)

IV.2 s.d. *Enter . . . Starveling* Enter Quince, Flute, Thisby and the rabble (QQ) Enter Quince, Flute, Thisbie, Snout, and Starueling (F)   3 *STARVELING* (F Staru.) Flut. (QQ)   5, 9, 13, 19 *FLUTE* Thys. or This. (QQ, F)

V.1 34 *our* (F) Or (Q1) or (Q2)   155 *Snout* (F) Flute (QQ)   190 *up in thee* (F) now againe (QQ)   193 *My love! thou art my love,* My loue thou art, my loue (QQ, F)   205 *mural down* Moon vsed (QQ) morall downe (F)   216 *beasts in, a* beasts, in a (QQ, F)   269 *gleams* beames (QQ, F)   306 *prove* (Q2, F) yet prooue (Q1)   307–8 *gone before Thisby* gone before? Thisby (QQ, F)   313 *mote* moth (QQ, F)   363 *lion* Lyons (QQ, F)   364 *behowls* beholds (Q, F)   411–12 these two lines transposed in QQ, F

A Midsummer Night's Dream

A Midsummer Night's Dream

❧ I.1 *Enter Theseus, Hippolyta, [Philostrate,] with others.*

THESEUS
    Now, fair Hippolyta, our nuptial hour
    Draws on apace. Four happy days bring in
    Another moon; but O, methinks, how slow
    This old moon wanes! She lingers my desires,   4
    Like to a stepdame or a dowager   5
    Long withering out a young man's revenue.
HIPPOLYTA
    Four days will quickly steep themselves in night,
    Four nights will quickly dream away the time,
    And then the moon, like to a silver bow
    New-bent in heaven, shall behold the night   10
    Of our solemnities.
THESEUS   Go, Philostrate,
    Stir up the Athenian youth to merriments,
    Awake the pert and nimble spirit of mirth,
    Turn melancholy forth to funerals:
    The pale companion is not for our pomp.   15
                                    [Exit Philostrate.]
    Hippolyta, I wooed thee with my sword,   16
    And won thy love doing thee injuries,

I.1 The duke's palace at Athens   4 *lingers* frustrates by delaying   5–6 *Like to a stepdame . . . revenue* (Theseus compares himself to a *young man* impatiently awaiting a diminished inheritance from a long-lived stepmother or widow)   15 *companion* fellow; *pomp* i.e., splendid marriage ceremony   16 *Hippolyta . . . sword* (one version of the Theseus myth records that he captured Hippolyta in his war against the Amazons)

But I will wed thee in another key,
19   With pomp, with triumph, and with reveling.
      Enter Egeus and his daughter Hermia, and Lysander
      and Demetrius.

EGEUS
20   Happy be Theseus, our renownèd duke.

THESEUS
21   Thanks, good Egeus. What's the news with thee?

EGEUS
      Full of vexation come I, with complaint
      Against my child, my daughter Hermia.
      Stand forth, Demetrius. My noble lord,
      This man hath my consent to marry her.
      Stand forth, Lysander. And, my gracious duke,
      This hath bewitched the bosom of my child.
      Thou, thou, Lysander, thou hast given her rhymes
      And interchanged love tokens with my child;
30   Thou hast by moonlight at her window sung
31   With feigning voice verses of feigning love,
32   And stol'n the impression of her fantasy
33   With bracelets of thy hair, rings, gauds, conceits,
34   Knacks, trifles, nosegays, sweetmeats – messengers
      Of strong prevailment in unhardened youth.
      With cunning hast thou filched my daughter's heart,
      Turned her obedience (which is due to me)
38   To stubborn harshness. And, my gracious duke,
      Be it so she will not here before your grace
40   Consent to marry with Demetrius,
      I beg the ancient privilege of Athens:
      As she is mine, I may dispose of her,
      Which shall be either to this gentleman
      Or to her death, according to our law
45   Immediately provided in that case.

---

19 *triumph* victorious procession **21** *Egeus* (pronounced "E-jée-us") **31**
feigning (1) longing ("faining"), (2) soft, (3) deceitful **32** *stol'n . . . fantasy*
secretly imprinted your image on her imagination (fancy) **33** *gauds* trin-
kets; *conceits* fanciful gifts or notions **34** *Knacks* knickknacks **38** *harshness*
i.e., hardness of heart **45** *Immediately* directly, without question

THESEUS
    What say you, Hermia? Be advised, fair maid.
    To you your father should be as a god,
    One that composed your beauties, yea, and one
    To whom you are but as a form in wax,
    By him imprinted, and within his power   *50*
    To leave the figure or disfigure it.   *51*
    Demetrius is a worthy gentleman.   *52*
HERMIA
    So is Lysander.
THESEUS   In himself he is;
    But in this kind, wanting your father's voice,   *54*
    The other must be held the worthier.
HERMIA
    I would my father looked but with my eyes.
THESEUS
    Rather your eyes must with his judgment look.
HERMIA
    I do entreat your grace to pardon me.
    I know not by what power I am made bold,
    Nor how it may concern my modesty   *60*
    In such a presence here to plead my thoughts,
    But I beseech your grace that I may know
    The worst that may befall me in this case
    If I refuse to wed Demetrius.
THESEUS
    Either to die the death, or to abjure
    For ever the society of men.
    Therefore, fair Hermia, question your desires,
    Know of your youth, examine well your blood,   68
    Whether, if you yield not to your father's choice,
    You can endure the livery of a nun,   70
    For aye to be in shady cloister mewed,   71

---

51 *To leave . . . it* to leave the image as it is or to destroy it **52** *worthy* noble
54 *in this kind* in this respect (as a suitor); *wanting . . . voice* lacking your father's approval **68** *blood* passions **70** *livery* habit **71** *aye* ever; *mewed* caged

To live a barren sister all your life,
73 Chanting faint hymns to the cold fruitless moon.
74 Thrice blessèd they that master so their blood
To undergo such maiden pilgrimage;
76 But earthlier happy is the rose distilled
Than that which, withering on the virgin thorn,
Grows, lives, and dies in single blessedness.

HERMIA
So will I grow, so live, so die, my lord,
80 Ere I will yield my virgin patent up
Unto his lordship whose unwishèd yoke
My soul consents not to give sovereignty.

THESEUS
Take time to pause, and by the next new moon –
The sealing day betwixt my love and me
For everlasting bond of fellowship –
Upon that day either prepare to die
For disobedience to your father's will,
Or else to wed Demetrius, as he would,
89 Or on Diana's altar to protest
90 For aye austerity and single life.

DEMETRIUS
Relent, sweet Hermia, and, Lysander, yield
92 Thy crazèd title to my certain right.

LYSANDER
You have her father's love, Demetrius,
Let me have Hermia's: do you marry him.

EGEUS
Scornful Lysander, true, he hath my love,
And what is mine my love shall render him,
And she is mine, and all my right of her
98 I do estate unto Demetrius.

---

73 *Chanting . . . moon* i.e., Hermia would become a priestess of Diana, virgin goddess of the moon   74–75 *Thrice blessèd . . . pilgrimage* (perhaps a compliment to Elizabeth, the Virgin Queen, thus softening the critique of virginity)   76 *distilled* i.e., made into perfume   80 *virgin patent* privilege of virginity   89 *protest* vow   92 *crazèd* cracked, faulty   98 *estate unto* bestow upon, will to (consistent with Egeus's description of Hermia as his property)

LYSANDER

   I am, my lord, as well derived as he,   99

   As well possessed; my love is more than his;   100

   My fortunes every way as fairly ranked

   (If not with vantage) as Demetrius';   102

   And (which is more than all these boasts can be)

   I am beloved of beauteous Hermia.

   Why should not I then prosecute my right?

   Demetrius – I'll avouch it to his head –   106

   Made love to Nedar's daughter, Helena,

   And won her soul, and she (sweet lady) dotes,

   Devoutly dotes, dotes in idolatry,

   Upon this spotted and inconstant man.   110

THESEUS

   I must confess that I have heard so much,

   And with Demetrius thought to have spoke thereof;

   But, being overfull of self-affairs,

   My mind did lose it. But, Demetrius, come,

   And come, Egeus. You shall go with me;

   I have some private schooling for you both.   116

   For you, fair Hermia, look you arm yourself   117

   To fit your fancies to your father's will;   118

   Or else the law of Athens yields you up

   (Which by no means we may extenuate)   120

   To death, or to a vow of single life.

   Come, my Hippolyta. What cheer, my love?

   Demetrius and Egeus, go along:

   I must employ you in some business

   Against our nuptial and confer with you   125

   Of something nearly that concerns yourselves.   126

EGEUS

   With duty and desire we follow you.

---

99 *well derived* well born   **100** *well possessed* wealthy   **102** *with vantage* even better   **106** *to his head* to his face   **110** *spotted* i.e., morally stained, untruthful   **116** *schooling* advice   **117** *look . . . yourself* see that you prepare **118** *fancies* affection (throughout the play "fancy" means both "imagination" and "love")   **120** *extenuate* mitigate, alter   **125** *Against* in advance of, concerning   **126** *nearly* closely (may modify *confer* or *concerns*)

Exeunt [all but Lysander and Hermia].

LYSANDER

How now, my love? Why is your cheek so pale?
How chance the roses there do fade so fast?

HERMIA

130   Belike for want of rain, which I could well
131   Beteem them from the tempest of my eyes.

LYSANDER

Ay me, for aught that I could ever read,
Could ever hear by tale or history,
The course of true love never did run smooth:
But either it was different in blood –

HERMIA

O cross! too high to be enthralled to low.

LYSANDER

137   Or else misgraffèd in respect of years –

HERMIA

O spite! too old to be engaged to young.

LYSANDER

139   Or merit stood upon the choice of friends –

HERMIA

140   O hell! to choose love by another's eyes.

LYSANDER

Or if there were a sympathy in choice,
War, death, or sickness did lay siege to it,
143   Making it momentany as a sound,
Swift as a shadow, short as any dream,
145   Brief as the lightning in the collied night,
146   That, in a spleen, unfolds both heaven and earth,
And ere a man hath power to say "Behold!"
The jaws of darkness do devour it up:
149   So quick bright things come to confusion.

---

130 *Belike* perhaps   131 *Beteem* allow, afford   137 *misgraffèd* ill-grafted, mismatched   139 *friends* relatives   143 *momentany* (common sixteenth-century form of "momentary," from Latin *momentaneus*)   145 *collied* murky (literally, blackened with coal dust)   146 *in a spleen* (1) on impulse, hence in a flash, (2) in a fit of fierce temper (the spleen was considered the seat of violent outbursts)   149 *quick* (1) quickly (adv.), (2) vital (adj.); *confusion* ruin

HERMIA

> If then true lovers have been ever crossed,   150
> It stands as an edict in destiny.   151
> Then let us teach our trial patience,   152
> Because it is a customary cross,   153
> As due to love as thoughts, and dreams, and sighs,
> Wishes, and tears, poor Fancy's followers.   155

LYSANDER

> A good persuasion. Therefore hear me, Hermia.
> I have a widow aunt, a dowager,
> Of great revenue, and she hath no child.   158
> From Athens is her house remote seven leagues,   159
> And she respects me as her only son.   160
> There, gentle Hermia, may I marry thee,
> And to that place the sharp Athenian law
> Cannot pursue us. If thou lovest me then,
> Steal forth thy father's house tomorrow night,
> And in the wood, a league without the town
> (Where I did meet thee once with Helena
> To do observance to a morn of May),   167
> There will I stay for thee.

HERMIA   My good Lysander,

> I swear to thee by Cupid's strongest bow,
> By his best arrow, with the golden head,   170
> By the simplicity of Venus' doves,   171
> By that which knitteth souls and prospers loves,   172
> And by that fire which burned the Carthage queen   173
> When the false Troyan under sail was seen,
> By all the vows that ever men have broke

---

151 *stands . . . destiny* can't be changed   152 *teach . . . patience* learn patience in this trial   153 *cross* obstacle, vexation   155 *poor Fancy's followers* sad courtiers to the monarch Love   158 *revenue* (here pronounced "revènue")   159 *seven leagues* "a long distance"   167 *observance . . . May* i.e., outdoor festivities associated with but not limited to May Day   170 *best . . . head* (Cupid's sharp golden arrow engenders love; his blunt leaden one causes dislike)   171 *simplicity* innocence, sincerity; *Venus' doves* (doves drew her chariot)   172 *prospers* nurtures, causes to flourish   173–74 *fire . . . seen* (Dido, Queen of Carthage, committed suicide on a funeral pyre when the Trojan Aeneas abandoned her to sail for Italy)

(In number more than ever women spoke),
In that same place thou hast appointed me
Tomorrow truly will I meet with thee.

LYSANDER
Keep promise, love. Look, here comes Helena.
Enter Helena.

HERMIA
180   God speed fair Helena. Whither away?

HELENA
Call you me fair? That "fair" again unsay.
182   Demetrius loves your fair. O happy fair!
183   Your eyes are lodestars, and your tongue's sweet air
More tuneable than lark to shepherd's ear
When wheat is green, when hawthorn buds appear.
186   Sickness is catching. O, were favor so,
Yours would I catch, fair Hermia; ere I go
My ear should catch your voice, my eye your eye,
My tongue should catch your tongue's sweet melody.
190   Were the world mine, Demetrius being bated,
191   The rest I'll give to be to you translated.
192   O, teach me how you look, and with what art
193   You sway the motion of Demetrius' heart.

HERMIA
I frown upon him, yet he loves me still.

HELENA
O that your frowns would teach my smiles such skill!

HERMIA
I give him curses, yet he gives me love.

HELENA
O that my prayers could such affection move!

HERMIA
The more I hate, the more he follows me.

---

180 *fair* beautiful (and implicitly blonde or light-complexioned, the Elizabethan standard of female beauty) 182 *your fair* i.e., your beautiful coloring
(Hermia is dark; see II.2.114) 183 *lodestars* guiding lights, like the polestar;
air music 186 *favor* appearance, especially good looks 190 *bated* excepted
191 *translated* transformed 192 *art* i.e., craft or magic (see I.1.27, 36)
193 *motion* tendency, affection

HELENA
　The more I love, the more he hateth me.
HERMIA
　His folly, Helena, is no fault of mine.   200
HELENA
　None but your beauty. Would that fault were mine!
HERMIA
　Take comfort. He no more shall see my face;
　Lysander and myself will fly this place.
　Before the time I did Lysander see,
　Seemed Athens as a paradise to me.
　O, then, what graces in my love do dwell
　That he hath turned a heaven unto a hell!
LYSANDER
　Helen, to you our minds we will unfold.
　Tomorrow night, when Phoebe doth behold   209
　Her silver visage in the wat'ry glass,   210
　Decking with liquid pearl the bladed grass
　(A time that lovers' flights doth still conceal),   212
　Through Athens' gates have we devised to steal.
HERMIA
　And in the wood where often you and I
　Upon faint primrose beds were wont to lie,   215
　Emptying our bosoms of their counsel sweet,   216
　There my Lysander and myself shall meet,
　And thence from Athens turn away our eyes
　To seek new friends and stranger companies.   219
　Farewell, sweet playfellow. Pray thou for us;   220
　And good luck grant thee thy Demetrius.
　Keep word, Lysander. We must starve our sight   222
　From lovers' food till morrow deep midnight.

---

200 *fault* (in early modern slang, *fault* was a term for the vagina or for forni-
cation; those secondary meanings may pertain here and at III.2.243)   209
Phoebe the moon, or Diana   212 *still* always   215 *faint* pale-colored; *wont*
accustomed   216 *counsel* secret plans, confidences   219 *stranger companies*
the company of strangers   222 *Keep word* i.e., don't break your promise

LYSANDER

    I will, my Hermia.   *Exit Hermia.*
             Helena, adieu.
    As you on him, Demetrius dote on you. *Exit Lysander.*

HELENA

226   How happy some o'er other some can be!
        Through Athens I am thought as fair as she.
        But what of that? Demetrius thinks not so;
        He will not know what all but he do know.
230   And as he errs, doting on Hermia's eyes,
231   So I, admiring of his qualities.
232   Things base and vile, holding no quantity,
        Love can transpose to form and dignity.
        Love looks not with the eyes, but with the mind,
        And therefore is winged Cupid painted blind.
236   Nor hath Love's mind of any judgment taste:
237   Wings, and no eyes, figure unheedy haste.
        And therefore is Love said to be a child,
        Because in choice he is so oft beguiled.
240   As waggish boys in game themselves forswear,
        So the boy Love is perjured everywhere.
242   For ere Demetrius looked on Hermia's eyne,
        He hailed down oaths that he was only mine;
        And when this hail some heat from Hermia felt,
        So he dissolved, and show'rs of oaths did melt.
        I will go tell him of fair Hermia's flight.
        Then to the wood will he tomorrow night
248   Pursue her; and for this intelligence
249   If I have thanks, it is a dear expense.
250   But herein mean I to enrich my pain,
251   To have his sight thither and back again.   *Exit.*

---

226 *other some* other people **231** *admiring of his qualities* marveling at his attractions, or "parts" **232** *holding no quantity* without proportion, therefore shapeless and unappealing **236** *Nor hath . . . taste* i.e., in matters of the heart, the imagination (*Love's mind*) has no trace of reason (*judgment*) **237** *figure* symbolize **240** *waggish* playful, teasing **242** *eyne* eyes (archaic plural) **248** *intelligence* secret information **249** *a dear expense* a costly but worthwhile effort **251** *his sight* the sight of him

*

❧ **I.2** *Enter Quince the Carpenter, and Snug the Joiner,*
and Bottom the Weaver, and Flute the Bellows Mender,
and Snout the Tinker, and Starveling the Tailor.

QUINCE   Is all our company here?

BOTTOM   You were best to call them generally, man by 2
man, according to the scrip. 3

QUINCE   Here is the scroll of every man's name which is
thought fit, through all Athens, to play in our interlude 5
before the duke and the duchess on his wedding day at
night.

BOTTOM   First, good Peter Quince, say what the play
treats on, then read the names of the actors, and so 9
grow to a point. 10

QUINCE   Marry, our play is "The most lamentable com- 11
edy and most cruel death of Pyramus and Thisby."

BOTTOM   A very good piece of work, I assure you, and a
merry. Now, good Peter Quince, call forth your actors
by the scroll. Masters, spread yourselves.

QUINCE   Answer as I call you. Nick Bottom the weaver.

BOTTOM   Ready. Name what part I am for, and proceed.

QUINCE   You, Nick Bottom, are set down for Pyramus.

BOTTOM   What is Pyramus? a lover, or a tyrant? 19

QUINCE   A lover that kills himself, most gallant, for love. 20

I.2 Peter Quince's house (?) **s.d.** (The names of the actors refer specifically to
their professions. *Quince* probably refers to "quoins" or "quines," wedge-
shaped pieces of wood used by carpenters. *Snug* implies the tightness of
joints required in cabinetry. *Bottom* is named for the reel on which the
weaver's thread is wound. *Flute* perhaps repairs the leather bellows that supply air to a flute organ. *Snout* refers to the spout of the kettle that a tinker
mends. *Starveling* is named for the proverbial skinniness of tailors.) **2** *gen-*
erally i.e., individually (here, as elsewhere, Bottom says the opposite of what
he means) **3** *scrip* list, script **5** *interlude* brief play, comedy **9** *treats on*
deals with, represents **11** *Marry* (a mild interjection diluted from an oath,
"By the Virgin Mary") **19** *lover . . . tyrant* (familiar leading roles in Elizabethan plays)

BOTTOM   That will ask some tears in the true performing of it. If I do it, let the audience look to their eyes. I
23 will move storms; I will condole in some measure. To
24 the rest. Yet my chief humor is for a tyrant. I could play
25 Ercles rarely, or a part to tear a cat in, to make all split.

> "The raging rocks
> And shivering shocks
> Shall break the locks
> Of prison gates,
30 > And Phibbus' car
> Shall shine from far
> And make and mar
> The foolish Fates."

This was lofty. Now name the rest of the players. This is
35 Ercles' vein, a tyrant's vein. A lover is more condoling.

QUINCE   Francis Flute the bellows mender.

FLUTE   Here, Peter Quince.

QUINCE   Flute, you must take Thisby on you.

39 FLUTE   What is Thisby? a wandering knight?

40 QUINCE   It is the lady that Pyramus must love.

41 FLUTE   Nay, faith, let not me play a woman. I have a
beard coming.

43 QUINCE   That's all one. You shall play it in a mask, and
you may speak as small as you will.

45 BOTTOM   An I may hide my face, let me play Thisby
too. I'll speak in a monstrous little voice: "Thisne,
Thisne!" "Ah, Pyramus, my lover dear, thy Thisby dear,
and lady dear!"

QUINCE   No, no, you must play Pyramus; and Flute, you
50 Thisby.

---

23 *condole* lament   **24** *humor* (1) temperament, (2) mood   **25** *Ercles* Hercules (a familiar ranting part, as in versions of Seneca's *Hercules Furens*); *to
tear . . . all split* (clichés for heroic, emotional parts)   **30** *Phibbus' car* the
chariot of Phoebus Apollo, the sun god (the mock-heroic style glances at English translations of Seneca)   **35** *condoling* pathetic, lamenting   **39** *wandering knight* knight-errant (another typical role)   **41** *faith* in faith, by my faith
(another mild oath)   **41–42** *I have . . . coming* i.e., I'm no longer a boy and so
can't play a woman   **43** *That's all one* it makes no difference   **45** *An* if

BOTTOM　Well, proceed.

QUINCE　Robin Starveling the tailor.

STARVELING　Here, Peter Quince.

QUINCE　Robin Starveling, you must play Thisby's 54
mother. Tom Snout the tinker.

SNOUT　Here, Peter Quince.

QUINCE　You, Pyramus' father; myself, Thisby's father;
Snug the joiner, you the lion's part. And I hope here is a
play fitted. 59

SNUG　Have you the lion's part written? Pray you, if it be, 60
give it me, for I am slow of study.

QUINCE　You may do it extempore, for it is nothing but 62
roaring.

BOTTOM　Let me play the lion too. I will roar that I will 64
do any man's heart good to hear me. I will roar that I
will make the duke say, "Let him roar again; let him
roar again."

QUINCE　An you should do it too terribly, you would
fright the duchess and the ladies, that they would
shriek; and that were enough to hang us all. 70

ALL　That would hang us, every mother's son.

BOTTOM　I grant you, friends, if you should fright the
ladies out of their wits, they would have no more dis- 73
cretion but to hang us; but I will aggravate my voice so 74
that I will roar you as gently as any sucking dove; I will 75
roar you an 'twere any nightingale. 76

QUINCE　You can play no part but Pyramus; for Pyramus
is a sweet-faced man, a proper man as one shall see in a 78
summer's day, a most lovely gentlemanlike man. Therefore you must needs play Pyramus. 80

54–57 *Thisby's mother, Pyramus' father, Thisby's father* (these characters do not
appear in the version performed in Act V; they do appear in Shakespeare's
source story)　59 *fitted* cast　62 *extempore* extemporaneously, off the top of
your head　64 *that* so that　73–74 *no more discretion* no choice　74 *aggravate* (again Bottom means the opposite – i.e., minimize, soften)　75 *roar
you* (a colloquialism suggesting "roar for you"; compare *your straw-color
beard* in ll. 84–85)　76 *an 'twere* as if it were　78 *proper* good-looking

BOTTOM   Well, I will undertake it. What beard were I
best to play it in?

QUINCE   Why, what you will.

84 BOTTOM   I will discharge it in either your straw-color
85 beard, your orange-tawny beard, your purple-in-grain
86 beard, or your French-crown-color beard, your perfit
yellow.

88 QUINCE   Some of your French crowns have no hair at all,
and then you will play barefaced. But masters, here are
90 your parts; and I am to entreat you, request you, and
91 desire you to con them by tomorrow night, and meet
me in the palace wood, a mile without the town, by
moonlight. There will we rehearse, for if we meet in the
94 city, we shall be dogged with company, and our devices
95 known. In the meantime I will draw a bill of properties,
such as our play wants. I pray you fail me not.

BOTTOM   We will meet, and there we may rehearse most
98 obscenely and courageously. Take pains, be perfit. Adieu.

QUINCE   At the Duke's Oak we meet.

100 BOTTOM   Enough. Hold, or cut bowstrings.   *Exeunt.*

*

～ **II.1** *Enter a Fairy at one door, and Robin Goodfellow*
[Puck] at another.

PUCK
How now, spirit, whither wander you?

84–86 *your . . . beard* (*your* is used colloquially to introduce items in a list, a
linguistic practice that survives today)   85 *orange-tawny* reddish or brownish
orange; *purple-in-grain* i.e., dyed deep red   86 *French-crown-color* golden
color of a French coin; *perfit* perfect   88 *French crowns* bald heads (syphilis,
"the French disease," caused hair loss)   90 *parts* (technical term for each
actor's personal script or part, containing only the lines and cues of his role);
am to have to   91 *con* learn by heart   94 *devices* schemes, purposes   95 *bill*
list   98 *obscenely* (error, perhaps a mixture of "obscurely" and "seemly," for
"privately"; perhaps Bottom's invention for "offstage," ob-scene); *be perfit*
i.e., know your lines perfectly   100 *Hold . . . bowstrings* (from archery, probably "do as you should or get out")
II.1 The wood outside Athens

FAIRY

Over hill, over dale,
   Thorough bush, thorough brier,   3
Over park, over pale,   4
   Thorough flood, thorough fire;   5
I do wander everywhere,
Swifter than the moon's sphere;   7
And I serve the Fairy Queen,
To dew her orbs upon the green.   9
The cowslips tall her pensioners be.   10
In their gold coats spots you see:
Those be rubies, fairy favors;
In those freckles live their savors.   13

I must go seek some dewdrops here,
And hang a pearl in every cowslip's ear.
Farewell, thou lob of spirits; I'll be gone.   16
Our queen and all her elves come here anon.

PUCK

The king doth keep his revels here tonight.
Take heed the queen come not within his sight.
For Oberon is passing fell and wrath,   20
Because that she, as her attendant, hath
A lovely boy, stolen from an Indian king;
She never had so sweet a changeling.   23
And jealous Oberon would have the child
Knight of his train, to trace the forests wild.   25
But she perforce withholds the lovèd boy,   26
Crowns him with flowers, and makes him all her joy.   27

---

3 *Thorough* (common two-syllable form of "through")   4 *pale* enclosed area (virtually synonymous with *park*)   5 *flood* water   7 *moon's* (as with "thorough," pronounced with two syllables, from the old possessive "moones")   9 *orbs* circles (here, fairy rings)   10 *pensioners* attendants (members of Queen Elizabeth's bodyguard, who wore splendid uniforms, were called "pensioners")   13 *savors* scent   16 *lob* lout or rustic (suggesting an adult spirit, as opposed to the child-fairy)   20 *passing fell and wrath* surpassingly fierce and angry   23 *changeling* (pronounced as three syllables: here, the child stolen by fairies; usually, the ugly child left to the human parents)   25 *trace* travel   26 *perforce* by force   27 *flowers* (pronounced as a monosyllable throughout)

And now they never meet in grove or green,
29 By fountain clear or spangled starlight sheen,
30 But they do square, that all their elves, for fear,
Creep into acorn cups and hide them there.

FAIRY
Either I mistake your shape and making quite,
33 Or else you are that shrewd and knavish sprite
34 Called Robin Goodfellow. Are not you he
35 That frights the maidens of the villagery,
36 Skim milk, and sometimes labor in the quern,
37 And bootless make the breathless housewife churn,
38 And sometime make the drink to bear no barm,
Mislead night wanderers, laughing at their harm?
40 Those that Hobgoblin call you, and sweet Puck,
You do their work, and they shall have good luck.
Are not you he?

PUCK   Thou speakest aright;
I am that merry wanderer of the night.
I jest to Oberon, and make him smile
When I a fat and bean-fed horse beguile,
Neighing in likeness of a filly foal;
47 And sometime lurk I in a gossip's bowl
48 In very likeness of a roasted crab,
And when she drinks, against her lips I bob
50 And on her withered dewlap pour the ale.
51 The wisest aunt, telling the saddest tale,
Sometime for three-foot stool mistaketh me:
Then slip I from her bum, down topples she,

---

29 *fountain* spring; *spangled starlight sheen* shining starlight   **30** *square* quarrel, square off   **33** *shrewd* mischievous (literally, evil or cursed)   **34** *Robin Goodfellow* (the proper name of this impish spirit, whose generic name is *Puck;* see note to l.40)   **35** *villagery* village folk   **36** *quern* hand grinder, for pepper, malt, etc.   **37** *bootless* in vain (because the liquid won't harden into butter); *housewife* (in Elizabethan times spelled "huswife" and pronounced "huss-if")   **38** *barm* head on the ale   **40** *Hobgoblin* Robin the goblin ("Hob" being a rural form of Robert or Robin); *Puck* (from Anglo-Saxon "puca")   **47** *gossip* old woman   **48** *crab* crab apple   **50** *dewlap* folds of skin around the throat   **51** *aunt* old lady; *saddest* most serious

And "tailor" cries, and falls into a cough,   54
And then the whole quire hold their hips and laugh,   55
And waxen in their mirth, and neeze, and swear   56
A merrier hour was never wasted there.
But room, fairy: here comes Oberon.   58

FAIRY
And here my mistress. Would that he were gone!
*Enter [Oberon,] the King of Fairies, at one door,
with his train; and the Queen [Titania], at another,
with hers.*

OBERON
Ill met by moonlight, proud Titania.   60

TITANIA
What, jealous Oberon? Fairies, skip hence.
I have forsworn his bed and company.

OBERON
Tarry, rash wanton. Am not I thy lord?   63

TITANIA
Then I must be thy lady; but I know
When thou hast stolen away from fairyland,
And in the shape of Corin sat all day,   66
Playing on pipes of corn, and versing love   67
To amorous Phillida. Why art thou here,
Come from the farthest steep of India,   69
But that, forsooth, the bouncing Amazon,   70
Your buskined mistress and your warrior love,   71
To Theseus must be wedded, and you come
To give their bed joy and prosperity?

---

54 *tailor* (proverbial shout for a fall, perhaps because tailors sat cross-legged on the floor to sew) **55** *quire* company, gathering **56** *waxen* increase; *neeze* sneeze **58** *But room, fairy* i.e., out of the way (Pope emends to "But make room") **63** *rash wanton* willful creature (*wanton* means "indiscriminate," implying its sexual sense of "lewd") **66–68** *Corin, Phillida* (conventional names for a shepherd and shepherdess in pastoral poetry) **67** *pipes of corn* flutes made of oat straw (*corn* is any kind of grain) **69** *steep* slope of a mountain (Q1 reads "steppe," perhaps the modern "step") **70** *bouncing* big, strapping (perhaps also "boasting") **71** *buskined* wearing buskins, leather leggings

OBERON

How canst thou thus, for shame, Titania,
75 Glance at my credit with Hippolyta,
Knowing I know thy love to Theseus?
Didst thou not lead him through the glimmering night
78 From Perigenia, whom he ravishèd?
And make him with fair Aegles break his faith,
80 With Ariadne, and Antiopa?

TITANIA

These are the forgeries of jealousy,
82 And never, since the middle summer's spring,
Met we on hill, in dale, forest, or mead,
84 By pavèd fountain or by rushy brook,
85 Or in the beachèd margent of the sea,
86 To dance our ringlets to the whistling wind,
But with thy brawls thou hast disturbed our sport.
Therefore the winds, piping to us in vain,
As in revenge, have sucked up from the sea
90 Contagious fogs which, falling in the land,
91 Hath every pelting river made so proud
92 That they have overborne their continents.
The ox hath therefore stretched his yoke in vain,
94 The plowman lost his sweat, and the green corn
Hath rotted ere his youth attained a beard;
The fold stands empty in the drownèd field,
97 And crows are fatted with the murrion flock;

---

75 *Glance at my credit with Hippolyta* mention my standing with Hippolyta
78–80 *Perigenia, Aegles, Ariadne, Antiopa* (a partial list of Theseus's mistresses
from Sir Thomas North's translation of Plutarch: *Perigenia* was the daughter
of Sinnis, slain by Theseus, who then seduced her [Plutarch calls her
"Perigouna"]; *Ariadne,* daughter of King Minos, helped him thread the
labyrinth and defeat the Minotaur; after escaping with her, Theseus abandoned Ariadne for *Aegles; Antiopa* is sometimes identified with Hippolyta, although here she is obviously another mistress) 82 *middle summer's spring*
beginning of midsummer (i.e., around June 21) 84 *pavèd fountain* spring
with pebbly bottom 85 *beachèd margent* shore, margin 86 *ringlets* dances
in a ring 91 *pelting* paltry 92 *continents* containing banks 94–95 *corn /
Hath rotted ere his youth attained a beard* grain has rotted before reaching maturity, with the obvious visual image, *beard* of silks 97 *murrion* afflicted
with murrain, a disease of sheep and cattle

The nine-men's morris is filled up with mud,   98
And the quaint mazes in the wanton green   99
For lack of tread are undistinguishable.   *100*
The human mortals want their winter cheer;   101
No night is now with hymn or carol blessed.   102
Therefore the moon, the governess of floods,   103
Pale in her anger, washes all the air,
That rheumatic diseases do abound.   105
And thorough this distemperature we see   106
The seasons alter: hoary-headed frosts
Fall in the fresh lap of the crimson rose,
And on old Hiems' thin and icy crown   109
An odorous chaplet of sweet summer buds   110
Is, as in mockery, set. The spring, the summer,
The childing autumn, angry winter change   112
Their wonted liveries; and the mazèd world,   113
By their increase, now knows not which is which.   114
And this same progeny of evils comes
From our debate, from our dissension;
We are their parents and original.

OBERON
Do you amend it then; it lies in you.
Why should Titania cross her Oberon?
I do but beg a little changeling boy   *120*
To be my henchman.   *121*

TITANIA   Set your heart at rest.

The world is a mess (handwritten marginal note)

---

98 *nine-men's morris* board game, which, when played outdoors, employed a
pattern cut in turf   99 *quaint mazes* tricky paths laid out for races; *wanton
green* uncontrolled growth   101 *winter cheer* (Theobald's emendation of
Q1's problematic "winter here"; whichever reading is chosen, the sense –
confirmed in the next line – is that the country folk must suffer the pains of
winter without the pleasures)   102 *hymn or carol* i.e., of the Christmas season   103 *Therefore* (as in ll. 88 and 93, "Because the fairies are quarreling");
floods tides   105 *That* so that; *rheumatic diseases* (1) colds and flu (diseases of
"rheum," or mucus), (2) rheumatism (*rheumatic* is pronounced with stress
on the first syllable, roughly like "lunatic")   106 *distemperature* disorder in
nature   109 *Hiems'. . . crown* the god of winter's head   110 *chaplet* garland
for the head   112 *childing* pregnant, bounteous   113 *wonted liveries* normal
garments; *mazèd* amazed, bewildered   114 *increase* produce, crops   121
henchman page

122 The fairyland buys not the child of me.
123 His mother was a vot'ress of my order,
And in the spicèd Indian air, by night,
Full often hath she gossiped by my side,
And sat with me on Neptune's yellow sands,
127 Marking th' embarkèd traders on the flood;
When we have laughed to see the sails conceive
129 And grow big-bellied with the wanton wind,
130 Which she, with pretty and with swimming gait
Following (her womb then rich with my young squire),
Would imitate, and sail upon the land
To fetch me trifles, and return again,
As from a voyage, rich with merchandise.
But she, being mortal, of that boy did die,
And for her sake do I rear up her boy,
And for her sake I will not part with him.

[margin handwritten: compares ships to the vot'ress]

OBERON
How long within this wood intend you stay?

TITANIA
Perchance till after Theseus' wedding day.
140 If you will patiently dance in our round
And see our moonlight revels, go with us.
142 If not, shun me, and I will spare your haunts.

OBERON
Give me that boy, and I will go with thee.

TITANIA
Not for thy fairy kingdom. Fairies, away!
145 We shall chide downright if I longer stay.
                    Exeunt [Titania and her train].

OBERON
Well, go thy way. Thou shalt not from this grove
147 Till I torment thee for this injury.

---

122 *The fairyland* i.e., all of fairyland   123 *vot'ress* votaress, woman who had
taken a vow to serve a deity   127 *Marking . . . flood* watching the trading
ships on the tide   129 *wanton* playful, amorous   140 *round* round dance
(cf. *ringlets,* II.1.86)   142 *shun, spare* (here synonymous)   145 *chide* brawl
147 *injury* insult

My gentle Puck, come hither. Thou rememb'rest
Since once I sat upon a promontory   149
And heard a mermaid, on a dolphin's back,   150
Uttering such dulcet and harmonious breath   151
That the rude sea grew civil at her song,   152
And certain stars shot madly from their spheres
To hear the sea-maid's music?
PUCK   I remember.
OBERON
    That very time I saw (but thou couldst not)
Flying between the cold moon and the earth
Cupid, all armed. A certain aim he took
At a fair vestal, thronèd by the west,   158
And loosed his love shaft smartly from his bow,   159
As it should pierce a hundred thousand hearts.   160
But I might see young Cupid's fiery shaft   161
Quenched in the chaste beams of the wat'ry moon,   162
And the imperial vot'ress passèd on,
In maiden meditation, fancy-free.   164
Yet marked I where the bolt of Cupid fell.   165
It fell upon a little western flower,
Before milk-white, now purple with love's wound,
And maidens call it love-in-idleness.   168
Fetch me that flower; the herb I showed thee once.
The juice of it, on sleeping eyelids laid,   *170*
Will make or man or woman madly dote   171
Upon the next live creature that it sees.
Fetch me this herb, and be thou here again

---

149 *Since* when; *promontory* a point of high land jutting into the sea   **150**
mermaid (equivalent to "siren" in early modern usage)   151 *dulcet* sweet;
breath voice, song   152 *civil* mannerly, gentle   158 *vestal* virgin priestess
(probably an allusion to Elizabeth, the Virgin Queen, here figured as a votaress of Diana, chaste goddess of the moon); *by the west* i.e., in England   159
love shaft Cupid's arrow   160 *As* as if   161 *I might see* I could see   162
wat'ry moon (see II.1.103)   164 *fancy-free* safe from thoughts of love   165
bolt arrow   168 *love-in-idleness* (another name for the pansy, from French
pensée, "meditation")   171 *or . . . or* either . . . or

174   Ere the leviathan can swim a league.

PUCK
  I'll put a girdle round about the earth
  In forty minutes.   *[Exit.]*

OBERON   Having once this juice,
  I'll watch Titania when she is asleep
178 And drop the liquor of it in her eyes.
  The next thing then she, waking, looks upon
180 (Be it on lion, bear, or wolf, or bull,
181 On meddling monkey, or on busy ape)
  She shall pursue it with the soul of love.
  And ere I take this charm from off her sight
  (As I can take it with another herb)
  I'll make her render up her page to me.
  But who comes here? I am invisible,
  And I will overhear their conference.
    Enter Demetrius, Helena following him.

DEMETRIUS
  I love thee not; therefore pursue me not.
  Where is Lysander and fair Hermia?
190 The one I'll slay, the other slayeth me.
  Thou told'st me they were stol'n unto this wood,
192 And here am I, and wood within this wood
  Because I cannot meet my Hermia.
  Hence, get thee gone, and follow me no more!

HELENA
195 You draw me, you hardhearted adamant!
196 But yet you draw not iron, for my heart
197 Is true as steel. Leave you your power to draw,
  And I shall have no power to follow you.

---

174 *leviathan* biblical sea monster, usually thought of as the whale 178 *liquor* liquid essence 181 *busy* meddlesome (as in "busybody") 192 *and wood* and mad (from a Germanic root for "raging" or "frantic") 195 *adamant* lodestone, magnet (the hardest stone, often confused with the diamond) 196–97 *But . . . steel* i.e., your magnetism attracts the finest metal, steel, rather than iron (the passage is full of puns on hardness, attraction, magnetism, and the violence associated with swords) 197 *Leave you* give up

DEMETRIUS

 Do I entice you? Do I speak you fair?
 Or rather do I not in plainest truth
 Tell you I do not nor I cannot love you?   *200*

HELENA

 And even for that do I love you the more.
 I am your spaniel, and Demetrius,
 The more you beat me, I will fawn on you.
 Use me but as your spaniel – spurn me, strike me,
 Neglect me, lose me; only give me leave,
 Unworthy as I am, to follow you.
 What worser place can I beg in your love –
 And yet a place of high respect with me –
 Than to be usèd as you use your dog?   *210*

DEMETRIUS

 Tempt not too much the hatred of my spirit,
 For I am sick when I do look on thee.

HELENA

 And I am sick when I look not on you.

DEMETRIUS

 You do impeach your modesty too much   *214*
 To leave the city and commit yourself
 Into the hands of one that loves you not,
 To trust the opportunity of night
 And the ill counsel of a desert place   *218*
 With the rich worth of your virginity.

HELENA

 Your virtue is my privilege. For that   *220*
 It is not night when I do see your face,
 Therefore I think I am not in the night,
 Nor doth this wood lack worlds of company,
 For you, in my respect, are all the world.   *224*
 Then how can it be said I am alone

she has lost her self-respect

---

214 *impeach* call in question, imperil **218** *desert* deserted, wild **220** *Your . . . privilege* your excellence gives me license; *For that* because **224** *re-spect* estimation

When all the world is here to look on me?

DEMETRIUS

227   I'll run from thee and hide me in the brakes
And leave thee to the mercy of wild beasts.

HELENA

The wildest hath not such a heart as you.

230   Run when you will. The story shall be changed:
Apollo flies and Daphne holds the chase,

232   The dove pursues the griffin, the mild hind
Makes speed to catch the tiger – bootless speed,
When cowardice pursues, and valor flies.

DEMETRIUS

235   I will not stay thy questions. Let me go!
Or if thou follow me, do not believe
But I shall do thee mischief in the wood.

HELENA

Ay, in the temple, in the town, the field
You do me mischief. Fie, Demetrius.

240   Your wrongs do set a scandal on my sex.
We cannot fight for love, as men may do;
We should be wooed, and were not made to woo.

                                        [Exit Demetrius.]

I'll follow thee, and make a heaven of hell
To die upon the hand I love so well.   *[Exit.]*

OBERON

Fare thee well, nymph. Ere he do leave this grove,
Thou shalt fly him, and he shall seek thy love.
    Enter Puck.
Hast thou the flower there? Welcome, wanderer.

PUCK

Ay, there it is.

OBERON   I pray thee give it me.

---

227 *brakes* thickets   230–31 *The story . . . chase* i.e., we will reverse the story
of Daphne (who fled Apollo's advances and was transformed into a laurel
tree)   232 *griffin* mythical winged creature with the head of an eagle and the
body of a lion; *hind* doe   235 *stay thy questions* wait for or endure further
conversation   240 *set a scandal on my sex* cause me to disgrace my gender

I know a bank where the wild thyme blows,   249
Where oxlips and the nodding violet grows,   250
Quite overcanopied with luscious woodbine,   251
With sweet musk roses, and with eglantine.   252
There sleeps Titania sometime of the night,   253
Lulled in these flowers with dances and delight;
And there the snake throws her enameled skin,
Weed wide enough to wrap a fairy in.   256
And with the juice of this I'll streak her eyes
And make her full of hateful fantasies.   258
Take thou some of it and seek through this grove.
A sweet Athenian lady is in love   260
With a disdainful youth. Anoint his eyes;
But do it when the next thing he espies
May be the lady. Thou shalt know the man
By the Athenian garments he hath on.
Effect it with some care, that he may prove
More fond on her than she upon her love;   266
And look thou meet me ere the first cock crow.

PUCK
Fear not, my lord; your servant shall do so.   *Exeunt.*

*

❧ **II.2** *Enter Titania, Queen of Fairies, with her train.*

TITANIA
Come, now a roundel and a fairy song;   1
Then, for the third part of a minute, hence:
Some to kill cankers in the musk-rose buds,   3
Some war with reremice for their leathern wings,   4

---

249 *blows* blooms   **250** *oxlips* (species of primrose similar to a cowslip) **251** *overcanopied* (modifies *bank*); *woodbine* honeysuckle (but also applied to different vines; cf. IV.1.41)   **252** *musk roses* large, fragrant roses; *eglantine* sweetbrier, a wild rose   **253** *sometime of* at some time during   **256** *Weed* garment   **258** *fantasies* fancies, affections   **266** *fond on* mad about, in love with
   II.2 Another part of the wood   **1** *roundel* (1) round dance (cf. *ringlets, round*, II.1.86, 140), (2) song with a refrain   **3** *cankers* worms, caterpillars **4** *reremice* bats

To make my small elves coats, and some keep back
The clamorous owl, that nightly hoots and wonders
7   At our quaint spirits. Sing me now asleep.
8   Then to your offices, and let me rest.
       Fairies sing.
[FIRST FAIRY]
9   You spotted snakes with double tongue,
10   Thorny hedgehogs, be not seen;
11   Newts and blindworms, do no wrong,
                Come not near our Fairy Queen.

       [Chorus]
13   Philomele, with melody
                Sing in our sweet lullaby,
            Lulla, lulla, lullaby; lulla, lulla, lullaby;
                Never harm
                Nor spell nor charm
            Come our lovely lady nigh.
            So good night, with lullaby.

       FIRST FAIRY
20   Weaving spiders, come not here:
                Hence, you long-legged spinners, hence!
            Beetles black, approach not near;
                Worm nor snail, do no offense.

       [Chorus]
                Philomele, with melody, etc.
       [She sleeps.]
       SECOND FAIRY
                Hence, away! Now all is well.
                One aloof stand sentinel.   *[Exeunt Fairies.]*
       Enter Oberon [and squeezes the flower onto Titania's
       eyelids].

       OBERON
                What thou seest when thou dost wake,

---

7 *quaint* fine, elegant   8 *offices* tasks   9 *double* forked   11 *Newts* poisonous
water lizards; *blindworms* small snakes   13 *Philomele* Ovid's Philomela,
raped by her brother-in-law and turned into a nightingale (*Metamorphoses*,
VI)

Do it for thy true love take;
Love and languish for his sake.
Be it ounce or cat or bear,   30
Pard, or boar with bristled hair,   31
In thy eye that shall appear   32
When thou wak'st, it is thy dear.
Wake when some vile thing is near.   *[Exit.]*
     Enter Lysander and Hermia.

LYSANDER
Fair love, you faint with wand'ring in the wood;
And to speak troth, I have forgot our way.   36
We'll rest us, Hermia, if you think it good,
And tarry for the comfort of the day.

HERMIA
Be it so, Lysander. Find you out a bed,
For I upon this bank will rest my head.   40

LYSANDER
One turf shall serve as pillow for us both,
One heart, one bed, two bosoms, and one troth.   42

HERMIA
Nay, good Lysander. For my sake, my dear,
Lie further off yet; do not lie so near.

LYSANDER
O, take the sense, sweet, of my innocence.   45
Love takes the meaning in love's conference.   46
I mean that my heart unto yours is knit,
So that but one heart we can make of it:
Two bosoms interchainèd with an oath,
So then two bosoms and a single troth.   50
Then by your side no bed room me deny,
For lying so, Hermia, I do not lie.

HERMIA
Lysander riddles very prettily.

---

30 *ounce* lynx **31** *Pard* leopard **32** *that* that which **36** *to speak troth* to tell the truth, frankly **42** *troth* faithful love **45** *take . . . innocence* recognize the innocence of my intentions **46** *Love . . . conference* when lovers talk, love should interpret the meaning appropriately

54 Now much beshrew my manners and my pride
    If Hermia meant to say Lysander lied.
56 But, gentle friend, for love and courtesy
57 Lie further off, in human modesty.
    Such separation as may well be said
    Becomes a virtuous bachelor and a maid,
60 So far be distant; and good night, sweet friend.
    Thy love ne'er alter till thy sweet life end.

LYSANDER
    Amen, amen, to that fair prayer say I,
    And then end life when I end loyalty.
    Here is my bed. Sleep give thee all his rest!

HERMIA
65 With half that wish the wisher's eyes be pressed!
        [They sleep.]
        Enter Puck.

PUCK
        Through the forest have I gone,
        But Athenian found I none
68   On whose eyes I might approve
        This flower's force in stirring love.
70   Night and silence! Who is here?
        Weeds of Athens he doth wear.
        This is he (my master said)
        Despisèd the Athenian maid;
        And here the maiden, sleeping sound
        On the dank and dirty ground.
        Pretty soul, she durst not lie
77   Near this lack-love, this kill-courtesy.
78   Churl, upon thy eyes I throw

---

54 *beshrew* curse (in a mild sense) 56 *courtesy* good manners 57 *human modesty* (Q1 and F print "humane modesty," and the adjective may carry the sense of "thoughtful") 60 *So far be distant* be just that distant (as propriety requires) 65 *With . . . wish* may you have half of *all* sleep's rest; *pressed* closed in sleep 68 *approve* test, put to proof 77 *this lack-love, this kill-courtesy* this hardhearted, insensitive man 78 *Churl* rude, unmannerly person (literally, "peasant")

All the power this charm doth owe: 79
[He squeezes the flower onto Lysander's eyelids.]
When thou wak'st, let love forbid   80
Sleep his seat on thy eyelid.
So awake when I am gone,
For I must now to Oberon.   *Exit.*
Enter Demetrius and Helena, running.

HELENA
Stay, though thou kill me, sweet Demetrius.

DEMETRIUS
I charge thee, hence, and do not haunt me thus.

HELENA
O, wilt thou darkling leave me? Do not so.   86

DEMETRIUS
Stay, on thy peril! I alone will go.   *[Exit.]*   87

HELENA
O, I am out of breath in this fond chase.   88
The more my prayer, the lesser is my grace.   89
Happy is Hermia, wheresoe'er she lies,   90
For she hath blessèd and attractive eyes.
How came her eyes so bright? Not with salt tears.
If so, my eyes are oft'ner washed than hers.
No, no! I am as ugly as a bear,
For beasts that meet me run away for fear.
Therefore no marvel though Demetrius
Do, as a monster, fly my presence thus.   97
What wicked and dissembling glass of mine   98
Made me compare with Hermia's sphery eyne?   99
But who is here? Lysander, on the ground?   100
Dead, or asleep? I see no blood, no wound.

---

79 *owe* own, possess   **80–81** *let love forbid / Sleep his seat on thy eyelid* let love make you sleepless (prevent *Sleep* from taking *his seat*)   **86** *darkling* in the dark   **87** *Stay, on thy peril!* don't follow me, or else   **88** *fond* foolish   **89** *grace* blessing, favorable answer   **97** *as a monster* i.e., as he would from a monster   **98** *glass* mirror   **99** *compare* (perhaps "compare myself with," but more probably "compete with, attempt to rival"); *sphery eyne* eyes as bright as stars in their spheres

Lysander, if you live, good sir, awake.

LYSANDER *[Starts up.]*
     And run through fire I will for thy sweet sake.
104 Transparent Helena, nature shows art,
     That through thy bosom makes me see thy heart.
     Where is Demetrius? O, how fit a word
     Is that vile name to perish on my sword!

HELENA
     Do not say so, Lysander, say not so.
109 What though he love your Hermia? Lord! what
        though?
110 Yet Hermia still loves you. Then be content.

LYSANDER
     Content with Hermia? No! I do repent
     The tedious minutes I with her have spent.
     Not Hermia, but Helena I love.
114 Who will not change a raven for a dove?
115 The will of man is by his reason swayed,
     And reason says you are the worthier maid.
     Things growing are not ripe until their season:
118 So I, being young, till now ripe not to reason.
119 And touching now the point of human skill,
120 Reason becomes the marshal to my will
121 And leads me to your eyes, where I o'erlook
     Love's stories, written in Love's richest book.

HELENA
     Wherefore was I to this keen mockery born?
     When at your hands did I deserve this scorn?
     Is't not enough, is't not enough, young man,
     That I did never, no, nor never can,

---

104 *Transparent* brilliant (but also the modern sense of "able to be seen through"); *nature shows art* i.e., nature displays her ingenuity and craftsmanship (in allowing me to see your heart) 109 *What though* so what if 114 *raven for a dove* (perhaps referring to Hermia's dark hair and complexion, III.2.257) 115 *will* desire (possibly with specific sexual sense: *will* could also mean "penis") 118 *ripe not* have not yet ripened 119 *touching . . . skill* i.e., reason reaching the height of its development 121 *o'erlook* survey, read

Deserve a sweet look from Demetrius' eye,
But you must flout my insufficiency?
Good troth, you do me wrong! good sooth, you do,   129
In such disdainful manner me to woo.   130
But fare you well. Perforce I must confess
I thought you lord of more true gentleness.   132
O, that a lady, of one man refused,
Should of another therefore be abused!   *Exit.*

LYSANDER
She sees not Hermia. Hermia, sleep thou there,
And never mayst thou come Lysander near.
For, as a surfeit of the sweetest things   137
The deepest loathing to the stomach brings,
Or as the heresies that men do leave   139
Are hated most of those they did deceive,   140
So thou, my surfeit and my heresy,
Of all be hated, but the most of me!
And, all my powers, address your love and might   143
To honor Helen and to be her knight.   *Exit.* 144

HERMIA   *[Awakes.]*
Help me, Lysander, help me! Do thy best
To pluck this crawling serpent from my breast.
Ay me, for pity. What a dream was here!
Lysander, look how I do quake with fear.
Methought a serpent eat my heart away,   149
And you sat smiling at his cruel prey.   150
Lysander! What, removed? Lysander! lord!
What, out of hearing gone? No sound, no word?
Alack, where are you? Speak, an if you hear.   153
Speak, of all loves! I swoon almost with fear.   154
No? Then I well perceive you are not nigh.
Either death, or you, I'll find immediately.   *Exit.*

*

---

129 *Good troth, good sooth* (emphatic phrases – "indeed")   132 *gentleness*
gentility, courtesy   137 *surfeit* excess   139 *leave* give up, renounce   143
address direct   144 *knight* true love, amorous servant   149 *eat* ate (pronounced "ĕt")   150 *prey* act of preying   153 *an if* if   154 *of all loves* by all
true love

∾ **III.1** *Enter the Clowns [Quince, Snug, Bottom, Flute, Snout, and Starveling].*

BOTTOM   Are we all met?

QUINCE   Pat, pat; and here's a marvelous convenient place for our rehearsal. This green plot shall be our
4   stage, this hawthorn brake our tiring house, and we will do it in action as we will do it before the duke.

BOTTOM   Peter Quince?

7   QUINCE   What sayest thou, bully Bottom?

BOTTOM   There are things in this comedy of Pyramus and Thisby that will never please. First, Pyramus must
10   draw a sword to kill himself, which the ladies cannot abide. How answer you that?

12   SNOUT   By'r lakin, a parlous fear.

STARVELING   I believe we must leave the killing out, when all is done.

BOTTOM   Not a whit. I have a device to make all well.
16   Write me a prologue, and let the prologue seem to say, we will do no harm with our swords, and that Pyramus is not killed indeed; and for the more better assurance, tell them that I Pyramus am not Pyramus, but Bottom
20   the weaver. This will put them out of fear.

QUINCE   Well, we will have such a prologue, and it shall
22   be written in eight and six.

BOTTOM   No, make it two more; let it be written in eight and eight.

III.1 s.d. *Enter the Clowns* (although the folio begins a new act, the continuous text in Q1 shows that there is no break and that the stage is not entirely cleared: Titania remains asleep, apart from the rehearsing mechanicals) **4** *brake* thicket or hedge; *tiring house* dressing room ("attiring house") **7** *bully* (here a term of affection meaning "gallant," "fine fellow") **12** *By'r lakin* (a diluted oath from "by our Lady" – i.e., the Virgin Mary); *parlous* perilous, serious **16** *Write me* i.e., write (a colloquialism, like *roar you*, I.2.75) **22** *eight and six* i.e., common ballad meter (alternating lines of eight and six syllables, or four and three stresses)

SNOUT   Will not the ladies be afeard of the lion?   25

STARVELING   I fear it, I promise you.

BOTTOM   Masters, you ought to consider with yourselves, to bring in (God shield us) a lion among ladies is
a most dreadful thing. For there is not a more fearful
wildfowl than your lion living, and we ought to look   30
to't.

SNOUT   Therefore another prologue must tell he is not a
lion.

BOTTOM   Nay, you must name his name, and half his
face must be seen through the lion's neck, and he himself must speak through, saying thus, or to the same de-
fect: "Ladies," or "Fair ladies, – I would wish you" or "I
would request you" or "I would entreat you – not to
fear, not to tremble. My life for yours! If you think I
come hither as a lion, it were pity of my life. No! I am   40
no such thing. I am a man as other men are." And
there, indeed, let him name his name and tell them
plainly he is Snug the joiner.

QUINCE   Well, it shall be so. But there is two hard things:
that is, to bring the moonlight into a chamber; for you
know, Pyramus and Thisby meet by moonlight.

SNOUT   Doth the moon shine that night we play our
play?

BOTTOM   A calendar, a calendar! Look in the almanac.
Find out moonshine, find out moonshine.   50

QUINCE   Yes, it doth shine that night.

BOTTOM   Why, then may you leave a casement of the
great chamber window, where we play, open, and the
moon may shine in at the casement.

---

25 *Will not . . . the lion?* (at the baptismal celebration of Prince Henry of
Scotland, August 30, 1594, a plan to have a chariot pulled by a lion was dis-
carded as too dangerous and unpredictable) **40** *it were . . . life* i.e., I
wouldn't for the life of me want you to think that

55 QUINCE   Ay. Or else one must come in with a bush of
56   thorns and a lantern, and say he comes to disfigure, or
57   to present, the person of Moonshine. Then there is an-
      other thing. We must have a wall in the great chamber;
      for Pyramus and Thisby, says the story, did talk
60   through the chink of a wall.

SNOUT   You can never bring in a wall. What say you,
      Bottom?

BOTTOM   Some man or other must present Wall; and let
64   him have some plaster, or some loam, or some rough-
      cast about him, to signify wall; and let him hold his fin-
      gers thus, and through that cranny shall Pyramus and
      Thisby whisper.

QUINCE   If that may be, then all is well. Come, sit down
      every mother's son, and rehearse your parts. Pyramus,
70   you begin. When you have spoken your speech, enter
      into that brake; and so every one according to his cue.
          Enter Robin [Puck].

PUCK
72   What hempen homespuns have we swagg'ring here,
      So near the cradle of the Fairy Queen?
74   What, a play toward? I'll be an auditor;
      An actor too perhaps, if I see cause.

QUINCE   Speak, Pyramus. Thisby, stand forth.

BOTTOM   *[As Pyramus]*
77   Thisby, the flowers of odious savors sweet —

QUINCE   Odorous, odorous.

BOTTOM   *[As Pyramus]*
      — odors savors sweet;
80   So hath thy breath, my dearest Thisby dear.
      But hark, a voice! Stay thou but here awhile,

55–56 *bush of thorns* bundle of sticks from a thornbush (the man in the
moon was traditionally supposed to have such a bundle and a dog; one legend held that he had been banished to the moon for stealing wood) 56 *disfigure* (blunder for "figure" – i.e., represent) 57 *present* play, represent (in
theatrical parlance) 64–65 *roughcast* mixture like plaster for covering walls
or buildings 72 *hempen homespuns* bumpkins dressed in coarse peasant garb
74 *toward* on the way 77 *of* (perhaps Bottom's pronunciation of "have")

And by and by I will to thee appear.   *Exit.*   82
PUCK

A stranger Pyramus than e'er played here!   *[Exit.]*
FLUTE   Must I speak now?
QUINCE   Ay, marry, must you. For you must understand
he goes but to see a noise that he heard, and is to come
again.
FLUTE   *[As Thisby]*
Most radiant Pyramus, most lily-white of hue,
    Of color like the red rose on triumphant brier,
Most bristly juvenile, and eke most lovely Jew,   90
    As true as truest horse, that yet would never tire,
I'll meet thee, Pyramus, at Ninny's tomb.
QUINCE   "Ninus' tomb," man. Why, you must not speak   93
that yet. That you answer to Pyramus. You speak all
your part at once, cues and all. Pyramus, enter. Your
cue is past; it is "never tire."
FLUTE   O – *[As Thisby]*   97
As true as truest horse, that yet would never tire.
[Enter Puck, and Bottom with the ass head.]
BOTTOM   *[As Pyramus]*
If I were fair, Thisby, I were only thine.   98
QUINCE   O monstrous! O strange! We are haunted. Pray,
masters! Fly, masters! Help!   100
                    [Exeunt all the Clowns but Bottom.]
PUCK

I'll follow you; I'll lead you about a round,   101
    Through bog, through bush, through brake, through
    brier.

---

82 *by and by* shortly, soon   **90** *bristly juvenile* bearded youth (an absurdity characteristic of the play-within-the-play); *eke* also (already archaic in the 1590s); *Jew* (a poetic joke; Quince's – the playwright's – desperate rhyme for *hue*)   **93** *Ninus' tomb* (In Ovid the lovers meet secretly at the tomb of Ninus, mythical founder of Nineveh. Legend holds that his wife, Semiramis, built the walls of Babylon, home of Pyramus and Thisby.)   **97 s.d.** *Enter Puck, and Bottom with the ass head* (this stage direction, adapted from the folio, indicates theatrical practice of the time – i.e., "*the* ass head" prepared for the production)   **98** *fair* good-looking; *were only* would be only   **101** *about a round* round about

Sometime a horse I'll be, sometime a hound,
104 A hog, a headless bear, sometime a fire;
And neigh, and bark, and grunt, and roar, and burn,
Like horse, hound, hog, bear, fire, at every turn. *Exit.*

BOTTOM Why do they run away? This is a knavery of
them to make me afeard.
 Enter Snout.

SNOUT O Bottom, thou art changed. What do I see on
110 thee?

BOTTOM What do you see? You see an ass head of your
own, do you? *[Exit Snout.]*
 Enter Quince.

113 QUINCE Bless thee, Bottom, bless thee! Thou art translated. *Exit.*

BOTTOM I see their knavery. This is to make an ass of
me, to fright me, if they could. But I will not stir from
this place, do what they can. I will walk up and down
here, and I will sing, that they shall hear I am not afraid.
 [Sings.]

119   The ouzel cock so black of hue,
120   With orange-tawny bill,
121   The throstle with his note so true,
122   The wren with little quill –

TITANIA *[Arising]*
What angel wakes me from my flowery bed?

BOTTOM *[Sings.]*
  The finch, the sparrow, and the lark,
125   The plainsong cuckoo gray,
126   Whose note full many a man doth mark,
127   And dares not answer nay.

---

104 *fire* will-o'-the-wisp   113–14 *translated* transformed (literally "gone over to the other side")   119 *ouzel* the English blackbird   120 *orange-tawny* reddish-brown   121 *throstle* song thrush, the mavis   122 *quill* song pipe made of a reed (a metonymy for the bird's song)   125 *plainsong* with a simple and repetitive song (like the traditional plainsong chant)   126 *mark* notice   127 *And dares not answer nay* i.e., the listener can't deny the cuckoo's implication of cuckoldry (perhaps with a homonym for the ass's "neigh")

For, indeed, who would set his wit to so foolish a bird?   128
Who would give a bird the lie, though he cry "cuckoo"
never so?   130

TITANIA
I pray thee, gentle mortal, sing again.
Mine ear is much enamored of thy note;
So is mine eye enthrallèd to thy shape;
And thy fair virtue's force perforce doth move me,   134
On the first view, to say, to swear, I love thee.

BOTTOM   Methinks, mistress, you should have little reason for that. And yet, to say the truth, reason and love
keep little company together nowadays. The more the
pity that some honest neighbors will not make them   139
friends. Nay, I can gleek, upon occasion.   140

TITANIA
Thou art as wise as thou art beautiful.

BOTTOM   Not so, neither; but if I had wit enough to get
out of this wood, I have enough to serve mine own
turn.

TITANIA
Out of this wood do not desire to go.
Thou shalt remain here, whether thou wilt or no.
I am a spirit of no common rate,   147
The summer still doth tend upon my state,   148
And I do love thee. Therefore go with me.
I'll give thee fairies to attend on thee,   150
And they shall fetch thee jewels from the deep,
And sing while thou on pressèd flowers dost sleep;
And I will purge thy mortal grossness so
That thou shalt like an airy spirit go.
Peaseblossom, Cobweb, Moth, and Mustardseed!   155

---

128 *would set his wit* would bother to respond **134** *thy . . . force* your manly
strength **139** *honest neighbors* (Bottom personifies "reason" and "love" as
people who don't get along and need friends to reconcile them) **140** *gleek*
wisecrack **147** *rate* rank **148** *still* always, continually; *doth tend upon*
serves **155** *Moth* i.e., probably Mote, a speck (both words were spelled
"moth" and pronounced "mote")

Enter four Fairies [Peaseblossom, Cobweb, Moth, and
Mustardseed].

PEASEBLOSSOM   Ready.

COBWEB
   And I.

MOTH   And I.

MUSTARDSEED   And I.

ALL   Where shall we go?

TITANIA
   Be kind and courteous to this gentleman.
   Hop in his walks and gambol in his eyes;
160   Feed him with apricocks and dewberries,
   With purple grapes, green figs, and mulberries.
162   The honey bags steal from the humblebees,
   And for night tapers crop their waxen thighs,
   And light them at the fiery glowworm's eyes,
   To have my love to bed and to arise;
   And pluck the wings from painted butterflies
   To fan the moonbeams from his sleeping eyes.
   Nod to him, elves, and do him courtesies.

PEASEBLOSSOM   Hail, mortal!

170 COBWEB   Hail!

MOTH   Hail!

MUSTARDSEED   Hail!

BOTTOM   I cry your worships mercy, heartily. I beseech
   your worship's name.

COBWEB   Cobweb.

BOTTOM   I shall desire you of more acquaintance, good
177   Master Cobweb. If I cut my finger, I shall make bold
   with you. Your name, honest gentleman?

PEASEBLOSSOM   Peaseblossom.

180 BOTTOM   I pray you, commend me to Mistress Squash,
181   your mother, and to Master Peasecod, your father.

---

160 *apricocks* apricots (early form); *dewberries* (probably blackberries, although some early writers consider the dewberry another form of goose-
berry)   162 *humblebees* bumblebees   177–78 *If . . . you* (cobweb was used
to stanch blood)   180 *Squash* an unripe peapod (i.e., not the familiar gourd)
181 *Peasecod* a ripe peapod

Good Master Peaseblossom, I shall desire you of more
acquaintance too. Your name, I beseech you, sir?

MUSTARDSEED   Mustardseed.

BOTTOM   Good Master Mustardseed, I know your pa-   185
tience well. That same cowardly, giantlike ox beef hath
devoured many a gentleman of your house. I promise
you your kindred hath made my eyes water ere now. I
desire you of more acquaintance, good Master Mustardseed.   190

TITANIA
    Come wait upon him; lead him to my bower.
        The moon, methinks, looks with a wat'ry eye,
And when she weeps, weeps every little flower,   193
        Lamenting some enforcèd chastity.   194
        Tie up my lover's tongue, bring him silently.
                    Exit [Titania with Bottom and Fairies].
                            *

∾ **III.2** *Enter [Oberon,] King of Fairies.*

OBERON
    I wonder if Titania be awaked;
    Then, what it was that next came in her eye,
    Which she must dote on in extremity.
        [Enter Puck.]
    Here comes my messenger. How now, mad spirit?
    What night rule now about this haunted grove?   5

PUCK
    My mistress with a monster is in love.
    Near to her close and consecrated bower,   7
    While she was in her dull and sleeping hour,   8
    A crew of patches, rude mechanicals   9
    That work for bread upon Athenian stalls,   10

185–86 *your patience* what you have had to endure   **193** *she weeps* i.e.,
causes dew   **194** *enforcèd* (1) violated by force, (2) involuntary
   III.2 The wood   **5** *night rule* disorder, revels   **7** *close* private   **8** *dull*
drowsy   **9** *patches* clowns, bumpkins; *rude mechanicals* rough, manual labor-
ers

Were met together to rehearse a play
Intended for great Theseus' nuptial day.

13   The shallowest thickskin of that barren sort,
14   Who Pyramus presented in their sport,
15   Forsook his scene and entered in a brake.
      When I did him at this advantage take,
17   An ass's nole I fixèd on his head.
      Anon his Thisby must be answerèd,
19   And forth my mimic comes. When they him spy, ·
20   As wild geese that the creeping fowler eye,
21   Or russet-pated choughs, many in sort,
      Rising and cawing at the gun's report,
      Sever themselves and madly sweep the sky,
      So at his sight away his fellows fly,
25   And at our stamp here o'er and o'er one falls;
      He "murder" cries and help from Athens calls.
      Their sense thus weak, lost with their fears thus strong,
28   Made senseless things begin to do them wrong,
      For briers and thorns at their apparel snatch:
30   Some, sleeves – some, hats; from yielders all things
      catch.
      I led them on in this distracted fear
32   And left sweet Pyramus translated there,
      When in that moment (so it came to pass)
      Titania waked, and straightway loved an ass.

OBERON
      This falls out better than I could devise.
36   But hast thou yet latched the Athenian's eyes

---

13 *thickskin* dull person; *barren sort* witless group   14 *presented* acted   15 *scene* stage   17 *nole* head (from "noddle"; cf. "noodle")   19 *mimic* burlesque actor or mime   20 *fowler* bird hunter   21 *russet-pated choughs* gray-headed jackdaws (russet was gray or reddish-brown homespun cloth); *in sort* in a flock   25 *at our stamp* (a disputed passage: the mythical Robin Goodfellow was known to stamp fiercely, but some editors follow Dr. Johnson's conjecture, "at a stump")   28 *Made senseless . . . wrong* they thought themselves attacked by inanimate objects   30 *from yielders all things catch* everything grabs at (or steals from) the fearful   32 *translated* transformed (as elsewhere)   36 *latched* moistened (from verbal form of "leak"; but perhaps "secured")

With the love juice, as I did bid thee do?

PUCK

I took him sleeping – that is finished too –
And the Athenian woman by his side,
That, when he waked, of force she must be eyed.   40

Enter Demetrius and Hermia.

OBERON

Stand close. This is the same Athenian.

PUCK

This is the woman, but not this the man.

DEMETRIUS

O, why rebuke you him that loves you so?
Lay breath so bitter on your bitter foe.

HERMIA

Now I but chide, but I should use thee worse,
For thou, I fear, hast given me cause to curse.
If thou hast slain Lysander in his sleep,
Being o'er shoes in blood, plunge in the deep,   48
And kill me too.
The sun was not so true unto the day   50
As he to me. Would he have stolen away
From sleeping Hermia? I'll believe as soon   52
This whole earth may be bored, and that the moon
May through the center creep, and so displease
Her brother's noontide with th' antipodes.
It cannot be but thou hast murdered him.
So should a murderer look – so dead, so grim.   57

DEMETRIUS

So should the murdered look, and so should I,
Pierced through the heart with your stern cruelty.

---

40 *That* so that; *of force she must be eyed* she will certainly be noticed **48**
Being o'er shoes i.e., having waded thus far, being already guilty **52–55** *I'll
believe as soon . . . antipodes* i.e., it's impossible: I could as easily believe that
the solid (*whole*) earth could be bored through, and that the moon (a
metonymy for "night") could pass through the opening, disrupting the sun-
shine (*Her brother's noontide*) and annoying those on the opposite side (*th'
antipodes*) **57** *dead* deadly

60 Yet you, the murderer, look as bright, as clear,
61 As yonder Venus in her glimmering sphere.

HERMIA
62 What's this to my Lysander? Where is he?
Ah, good Demetrius, wilt thou give him me?

DEMETRIUS
I had rather give his carcass to my hounds.

HERMIA
Out, dog! out, cur! Thou driv'st me past the bounds
Of maiden's patience. Hast thou slain him then?
Henceforth be never numbered among men.
O, once tell true: tell true, even for my sake.
Durst thou have looked upon him, being awake?
70 And hast thou killed him sleeping? O brave touch!
Could not a worm, an adder, do so much?
An adder did it; for with doubler tongue
Than thine, thou serpent, never adder stung.

DEMETRIUS
74 You spend your passion on a misprised mood.
I am not guilty of Lysander's blood,
Nor is he dead, for aught that I can tell.

HERMIA
I pray thee, tell me then that he is well.

DEMETRIUS
78 An if I could, what should I get therefor?

HERMIA
A privilege never to see me more;
80 And from thy hated presence part I so.
See me no more, whether he be dead or no.   *Exit.*

DEMETRIUS
There is no following her in this fierce vein.
Here therefore for a while I will remain.

---

61 *sphere* orbit in which the planet moved (a technical term from Ptolemaic astronomy)   **62** *What's this to* what does this have to do with   **70** *brave touch* noble stroke (ironic)   **74** *on a misprised mood* in mistaken anger   **78** *An if* if

So sorrow's heaviness doth heavier grow   84
For debt that bankrout sleep doth sorrow owe;   85
Which now in some slight measure it will pay,
If for his tender here I make some stay.   87
    Lie down [and sleep].

OBERON
What hast thou done? Thou hast mistaken quite
And laid the love juice on some true love's sight.
Of thy misprision must perforce ensue   90
Some true love turned, and not a false turned true.

PUCK
Then fate o'errules, that, one man holding troth,   92
A million fail, confounding oath on oath.

OBERON
About the wood, go swifter than the wind,
And Helena of Athens look thou find.
All fancy-sick she is, and pale of cheer   96
With sighs of love, that costs the fresh blood dear.   97
By some illusion see thou bring her here.
I'll charm his eyes against she do appear.   99

PUCK
I go, I go, look how I go,   *100*
Swifter than arrow from the Tartar's bow.   *[Exit.]*   *101*

84–85 *sorrow's heaviness . . . sorrow owe* (Demetrius says that his sorrow has become even more intense for lack of sleep: "heavy" means both "sad" and "drowsy")   **85** *bankrout* bankrupt (an early form, retained in this edition for its sound; the word establishes the legal discourse running through the end of the speech   **87** *If for . . . stay* (sleep has made an offer – *tender* – that will begin to repay his debt, and Demetrius will stop here – *make some stay* – to accept it); s.d. *Lie down [and sleep]* (an imperative form of stage direction common in Elizabethan plays)   **90** *misprision* error, misunderstanding   **92–93** *Then . . . on oath* then fate must have taken over, since for every man who is faithful (*holding troth*), a million are breaking (*confounding*) their promises   **96** *fancy-sick* lovesick; *cheer* face, look   **97** *that . . . dear* (each sigh was thought to extract a drop of blood from the heart)   **99** *against she do appear* in anticipation of her arrival   **101** *Tartar's bow* famously strong Oriental bow

OBERON

102   Flower of this purple dye,
                 Hit with Cupid's archery,
104   Sink in apple of his eye!

[He squeezes the flower onto Demetrius's eyelids.]
                 When his love he doth espy,
                 Let her shine as gloriously
                 As the Venus of the sky.
                 When thou wak'st, if she be by,
                 Beg of her for remedy.

Enter Puck.

PUCK

110   Captain of our fairy band,
                 Helena is here at hand,
                 And the youth, mistook by me,
113   Pleading for a lover's fee.
114   Shall we their fond pageant see?
                 Lord, what fools these mortals be!

OBERON

                 Stand aside. The noise they make
                 Will cause Demetrius to awake.

PUCK

                 Then will two at once woo one:
119   That must needs be sport alone.
120   And those things do best please me
121   That befall prepost'rously.

[They withdraw.]
Enter Lysander and Helena.

LYSANDER

Why should you think that I should woo in scorn?
         Scorn and derision never come in tears.
         Look, when I vow, I weep; and vows so born,

102–9 *dye . . . remedy* (all these "y" sounds were probably pronounced similarly, making eight rhymes on the same sound)   **104** *apple of his eye* pupil
113 *lover's fee* payment (e.g., kisses)   **114** *fond pageant* foolish performance
119 *alone* unmatched   **121** *prepost'rously* back to front, ass-backward

In their nativity all truth appears.
How can these things in me seem scorn to you,
Bearing the badge of faith to prove them true?   127

HELENA
You do advance your cunning more and more.   128
    When truth kills truth, O devilish-holy fray!   129
These vows are Hermia's. Will you give her o'er?   *130*
    Weigh oath with oath, and you will nothing weigh.
Your vows to her and me, put in two scales,
Will even weigh; and both as light as tales.   133

LYSANDER
I had no judgment when to her I swore.

HELENA
Nor none, in my mind, now you give her o'er.

LYSANDER
Demetrius loves her; and he loves not you.   136

DEMETRIUS   *[Awakes.]*
O Helen, goddess, nymph, perfect, divine!
To what, my love, shall I compare thine eyne?
Crystal is muddy. O, how ripe in show
Thy lips, those kissing cherries, tempting grow!   *140*
That pure congealèd white, high Taurus' snow,   141
Fanned with the eastern wind, turns to a crow   142
When thou hold'st up thy hand. O, let me kiss
This princess of pure white, this seal of bliss.   144

HELENA
O spite! O hell! I see you all are bent
To set against me for your merriment.
If you were civil and knew courtesy,   147

---

127 *badge of faith* (servants wore badges; for Lysander, the tears *prove* his allegiance to Helena) 128 *advance* display 129 *truth kills truth* one vow
cancels another; *devilish-holy fray* paradoxically, a holy war 133 *tales* false-
hoods, fictions 136 (Some editors, noticing the break in rhymed couplets,
posit a missing line here; others regard the broken rhyme scheme as deliber-
ate.) 141 *Taurus'* the Taurus Mountains in Turkey 142 *Fanned with* (1)
blown gently by, (2) winnowed by 144 *This . . . white* i.e., Helena's hand,
outclassing all others in whiteness 147 *civil* civilized

148   You would not do me thus much injury.
      Can you not hate me, as I know you do,
150   But you must join in souls to mock me too?
      If you were men, as men you are in show,
152   You would not use a gentle lady so,
153   To vow, and swear, and superpraise my parts,
      When I am sure you hate me with your hearts.
      You both are rivals, and love Hermia,
      And now both rivals to mock Helena.
157   A trim exploit, a manly enterprise,
      To conjure tears up in a poor maid's eyes
      With your derision! None of noble sort
160   Would so offend a virgin and extort
      A poor soul's patience, all to make you sport.

LYSANDER
      You are unkind, Demetrius. Be not so!
      For you love Hermia: this you know I know.
      And here, with all good will, with all my heart,
      In Hermia's love I yield you up my part;
      And yours of Helena to me bequeath,
      Whom I do love, and will do till my death.

HELENA
168   Never did mockers waste more idle breath.

DEMETRIUS
      Lysander, keep thy Hermia: I will none.
170   If e'er I loved her, all that love is gone.
171   My heart to her but as guestwise sojourned,
      And now to Helen is it home returned,
      There to remain.
LYSANDER   Helen, it is not so.

DEMETRIUS
      Disparage not the faith thou dost not know,
175   Lest, to thy peril, thou aby it dear.

---

148 *injury* insult   152 *gentle* (1) wellborn, (2) mild-mannered   153 *super-praise my parts* i.e., exaggerate my attractions   157 *trim* fine (ironic)   160 *extort* twist, torture   168 *idle* pointless   171 *My . . . sojourned* i.e., my heart visited Hermia only temporarily   175 *thou aby it dear* you have to pay (*aby*) a high price

Look where thy love comes. Yonder is thy dear.
Enter Hermia.

HERMIA

Dark night, that from the eye his function takes,   177
The ear more quick of apprehension makes.
Wherein it doth impair the seeing sense,
It pays the hearing double recompense.   180
Thou art not by mine eye, Lysander, found;
Mine ear, I thank it, brought me to thy sound.
But why unkindly didst thou leave me so?

LYSANDER

Why should he stay whom love doth press to go?

HERMIA

What love could press Lysander from my side?

LYSANDER

Lysander's love, that would not let him bide:
Fair Helena, who more engilds the night
Than all yon fiery oes and eyes of light.   188
Why seek'st thou me? Could not this make thee know,
The hate I bare thee made me leave thee so?   190

HERMIA

You speak not as you think. It cannot be.

HELENA

Lo, she is one of this confederacy.
Now I perceive they have conjoined all three
To fashion this false sport in spite of me.   194
Injurious Hermia, most ungrateful maid,   195
Have you conspired, have you with these contrived
To bait me with this foul derision?   197
Is all the counsel that we two have shared,   198
The sister's vows, the hours that we have spent
When we have chid the hasty-footed time   200

---

177 *his* its (common neuter possessive in Shakespeare's English); *takes* takes
away   188 *oes* round spangles (i.e., stars – with puns on "ohs" and "ays" in
oes and *eyes*)   190 *bare* (original past tense of "bear"; Shakespeare uses both
"bare" and the modern "bore")   194 *in spite of me* to spite me   195 *Injurious* insulting   197 *bait* torment (literally, to set on dogs to bite, as in bear-
baiting)   198 *counsel* secrets   200 *chid* criticized (past tense of "chide")

For parting us – O, is all forgot?
All schooldays' friendship, childhood innocence?
203   We, Hermia, like two artificial gods,
204   Have with our needles created both one flower,
Both on one sampler, sitting on one cushion,
Both warbling of one song, both in one key;
As if our hands, our sides, voices, and minds
208   Had been incorporate. So we grew together,
Like to a double cherry, seeming parted,
210   But yet an union in partition,
Two lovely berries molded on one stem.
So, with two seeming bodies, but one heart;
213   Two of the first, like coats in heraldry,
Due but to one, and crownèd with one crest.
215   And will you rent our ancient love asunder,
To join with men in scorning your poor friend?
It is not friendly, 'tis not maidenly.
Our sex, as well as I, may chide you for it,
Though I alone do feel the injury.

HERMIA
220   I am amazèd at your passionate words.
I scorn you not. It seems that you scorn me.

HELENA
Have you not set Lysander, as in scorn,
To follow me and praise my eyes and face?
And made your other love, Demetrius
225   (Who even but now did spurn me with his foot),
To call me goddess, nymph, divine, and rare,
Precious, celestial? Wherefore speaks he this
To her he hates? And wherefore doth Lysander
Deny your love, so rich within his soul,

---

203 *artificial* creating, skillful in artifice   **204** *needles* (pronounced "neeles,"
and often so spelled)   **208** *incorporate* in one body   **213–14** *Two . . . crest* (a
complex metaphor, in which the two girls are represented by the identical
sections of a heraldic shield: *the first* is a technical term for the first color or
quarter of a shield, and Helena imagines a shield with a repeated coat of arms
surmounted by a single crest, analogous to the *double cherry* on *one stem* in ll.
209–11)   **215** *rent* tear   **225** *even* (pronounced "e'en")

And tender me, forsooth, affection,   230
But by your setting on, by your consent?   231
What though I be not so in grace as you,   232
So hung upon with love, so fortunate,
But miserable most, to love unloved?
This you should pity rather than despise.

HERMIA
I understand not what you mean by this.

HELENA
Ay, do. Persever, counterfeit sad looks,   237
Make mouths upon me when I turn my back,
Wink each at other, hold the sweet jest up.
This sport, well carried, shall be chronicled.   *240*
If you have any pity, grace, or manners,
You would not make me such an argument.   242
But fare ye well. 'Tis partly my own fault,
Which death or absence soon shall remedy.

LYSANDER
Stay, gentle Helena, hear my excuse,
My love, my life, my soul, fair Helena!

HELENA
O excellent!

HERMIA   Sweet, do not scorn her so.

DEMETRIUS
If she cannot entreat, I can compel.   248

LYSANDER
Thou canst compel no more than she entreat.
Thy threats have no more strength than her weak   *250*
  prayers.
Helen, I love thee; by my life, I do!
I swear by that which I will lose for thee
To prove him false that says I love thee not.

---

230 *tender* offer   231 *setting on* prompting   232 *grace* favor   237 *Ay, do.
Persever* i.e., great, keep it up (Pronounced "persèver." The early texts read "I
doe," suggesting a response to Hermia's claim not to understand.)   242 *argument* theme or butt of a joke   248 *If . . . compel* i.e., if Helena can't succeed by pleading, I can force you to stop (scorning her)

DEMETRIUS
> I say I love thee more than he can do.

LYSANDER
> If thou say so, withdraw and prove it too.

DEMETRIUS
> Quick, come!

HERMIA   Lysander, whereto tends all this?

LYSANDER
257 Away, you Ethiope!

DEMETRIUS   No, no, sir, yield.
> Seem to break loose, take on as you would follow,
> But yet come not. You are a tame man, go!

LYSANDER *[To Hermia]*
260 Hang off, thou cat, thou burr! Vile thing, let loose,
> Or I will shake thee from me like a serpent.

HERMIA
> Why are you grown so rude? What change is this,
263 Sweet love?

LYSANDER   Thy love? Out, tawny Tartar, out!
264 Out, loathèd med'cine! O hated potion, hence!

HERMIA
265 Do you not jest?

HELENA   Yes, sooth! and so do you.

LYSANDER
> Demetrius, I will keep my word with thee.

DEMETRIUS
267 I would I had your bond, for I perceive
268 A weak bond holds you. I'll not trust your word.

LYSANDER
> What, should I hurt her, strike her, kill her dead?
270 Although I hate her, I'll not harm her so.

---

257 *Ethiope* (a dig at Hermia's dark coloring; the quarrel is degenerating into ethnic slurs, as in *tawny Tartar,* l. 263); *No, no, sir, yield* (Gary Taylor's convincing solution to a notorious crux. Q1 reads "No, no: heele [he'll?]"; F prints "No, no, Sir.")   263 *Out* Away! get out!   264 *med'cine, potion* (common synonyms for "poison")   265 *sooth* in truth   267 *your bond* your promise (with pun on "chain" in the following line)   268 *weak bond* i.e., Hermia's arms

HERMIA

    What, can you do me greater harm than hate?
    Hate me? Wherefore? O me, what news, my love?   272
    Am not I Hermia? Are not you Lysander?
    I am as fair now as I was erewhile.
    Since night you loved me, yet since night you left me.
    Why then you left me – O, the gods forbid! –
    In earnest, shall I say?

LYSANDER   Ay, by my life!
    And never did desire to see thee more.
    Therefore be out of hope, of question, of doubt;
    Be certain. Nothing truer. 'Tis no jest   280
    That I do hate thee and love Helena.

HERMIA   *[To Helena]*

    O me! You juggler, you canker blossom,   282
    You thief of love! What, have you come by night
    And stol'n my love's heart from him?

HELENA   Fine, i' faith.
    Have you no modesty, no maiden shame,
    No touch of bashfulness? What, will you tear
    Impatient answers from my gentle tongue?
    Fie, fie, you counterfeit, you puppet you!   288

HERMIA

    Puppet? Why, so! Ay, that way goes the game.   289
    Now I perceive that she hath made compare   290
    Between our statures; she hath urged her height,
    And with her personage, her tall personage,   292
    Her height, forsooth, she hath prevailed with him.
    And are you grown so high in his esteem
    Because I am so dwarfish and so low?   295
    How low am I, thou painted maypole? Speak!   296
    How low am I? I am not yet so low

---

272 *what news, my love* i.e., what's the trouble 282 *juggler* cheater, trickster (pronounced with three syllables); *canker blossom* worm that destroys (cankers) a blossom 288 *puppet* (1) counterfeit human, doll, (2) miniature person 289 *that . . . game* i.e., now I get it 292 *personage* personal appearance, figure 295 *low* short 296 *painted maypole* i.e., tall and skinny, with the implication that Helena's light complexion is cosmetically enhanced

But that my nails can reach unto thine eyes.

HELENA

I pray you, though you mock me, gentlemen,
300   Let her not hurt me. I was never curst.
I have no gift at all in shrewishness.
302   I am a right maid for my cowardice.
Let her not strike me. You perhaps may think,
Because she is something lower than myself,
305   That I can match her.

HERMIA   Lower? Hark again!

HELENA

Good Hermia, do not be so bitter with me.
I evermore did love you, Hermia,
Did ever keep your counsels, never wronged you,
Save that, in love unto Demetrius,
310   I told him of your stealth unto this wood.
He followed you; for love I followed him.
But he hath chid me hence, and threatened me
To strike me, spurn me, nay, to kill me too.
314   And now, so you will let me quiet go,
To Athens will I bear my folly back
And follow you no further. Let me go.
317   You see how simple and how fond I am.

HERMIA

Why, get you gone. Who is't that hinders you?

HELENA

A foolish heart, that I leave here behind.

HERMIA

320   What, with Lysander?

HELENA   With Demetrius.

LYSANDER

Be not afraid. She shall not harm thee, Helena.

DEMETRIUS

No, sir, she shall not, though you take her part.

---

300 *curst* shrewish, quarrelsome   302 *right* regular, real   305 *match her* i.e.,
in a fight   314 *so* if only   317 *fond* foolish

HELENA

  O, when she is angry, she is keen and shrewd.   323
  She was a vixen when she went to school,
  And though she be but little, she is fierce.

HERMIA

  "Little" again? nothing but "low" and "little"?
  Why will you suffer her to flout me thus?   327
  Let me come to her.

LYSANDER   Get you gone, you dwarf!
  You minimus, of hind'ring knotgrass made!   329
  You bead, you acorn!   *330*

DEMETRIUS   You are too officious
  In her behalf that scorns your services.
  Let her alone. Speak not of Helena;
  Take not her part. For if thou dost intend
  Never so little show of love to her,
  Thou shalt aby it.

LYSANDER   Now she holds me not.
  Now follow, if thou dar'st, to try whose right,
  Of thine or mine, is most in Helena.

DEMETRIUS

  Follow? Nay, I'll go with thee, cheek by jowl.
                [Exeunt Lysander and Demetrius.]

HERMIA

  You, mistress, all this coil is long of you.   339
  Nay, go not back.   *340*

HELENA   I will not trust you, I,
  Nor longer stay in your curst company.   341
  Your hands than mine are quicker for a fray;
  My legs are longer, though, to run away.

HERMIA

  I am amazed, and know not what to say.   344
                  Exeunt [Helena and Hermia].

---

323 *keen and shrewd* sharp and shrewish   **327** *suffer her to flout me* allow her to mock me   **329** *minimus* tiny thing; *knotgrass* low-growing plant that hinders the plow and was thought to stunt growth   **339** *coil is long of you* uproar is your fault   **341** *curst* contentious   **344** *amazed* bewildered (as in a maze)

OBERON   *[Coming forward]*
> This is thy negligence. Still thou mistak'st,
> Or else committ'st thy knaveries willfully.

PUCK
> Believe me, king of shadows, I mistook.
> Did not you tell me I should know the man
> By the Athenian garments he had on?

350
> And so far blameless proves my enterprise
> That I have 'nointed an Athenian's eyes;

352
> And so far am I glad it so did sort
> As this their jangling I esteem a sport.

OBERON
> Thou seest these lovers seek a place to fight.
> Hie therefore, Robin, overcast the night.

356
> The starry welkin cover thou anon

357
> With drooping fog as black as Acheron,
> And lead these testy rivals so astray
> As one come not within another's way.

360
> Like to Lysander sometime frame thy tongue,

361
> Then stir Demetrius up with bitter wrong,
> And sometime rail thou like Demetrius.
> And from each other look thou lead them thus
> Till o'er their brows death-counterfeiting sleep

365
> With leaden legs and batty wings doth creep.

366
> Then crush this herb into Lysander's eye,

367
> Whose liquor hath this virtuous property,

368
> To take from thence all error with his might

369
> And make his eyeballs roll with wonted sight.

370
> When they next wake, all this derision

371
> Shall seem a dream and fruitless vision,

---

352 *so did sort* happened this way   356 *welkin* sky   357 *Acheron* Hades
(from the name of one of its rivers)   361 *wrong* insults   365 *batty* batlike
366 *this herb* the antidote to the love-in-idleness applied earlier   367 *liquor*
essence; *virtuous* powerful   368 *his might* its power   369 *wonted* accustomed, normal   370 *derision* ridiculous behavior (pronounced with four syllables)   371 *fruitless* inconsequential, worthless

And back to Athens shall the lovers wend
With league whose date till death shall never end.   373
Whiles I in this affair do thee employ,
I'll to my queen and beg her Indian boy;
And then I will her charmèd eye release
From monster's view, and all things shall be peace.

PUCK
My fairy lord, this must be done with haste,
For night's swift dragons cut the clouds full fast,   379
And yonder shines Aurora's harbinger,   380
At whose approach ghosts, wand'ring here and there,
Troop home to churchyards. Damnèd spirits all,   382
That in crossways and floods have burial,
Already to their wormy beds are gone;
For fear lest day should look their shames upon,
They willfully themselves exile from light,
And must for aye consort with black-browed night.   387

OBERON
But we are spirits of another sort.
I with the Morning's love have oft made sport,   389
And, like a forester, the groves may tread   390
Even till the eastern gate, all fiery red,
Opening on Neptune, with fair blessèd beams
Turns into yellow gold his salt green streams.
But notwithstanding, haste; make no delay.
We may effect this business yet ere day.   *[Exit.]*

PUCK
                    Up and down, up and down,
                    I will lead them up and down.

---

373 *league whose date* agreement whose term or duration   379 *night's swift dragons* the mythical creatures thought to pull the chariot of the goddess of night   380 *Aurora's harbinger* the morning star, sign of dawn   382–83 *Damnèd spirits . . . burial* the ghosts of suicides, buried at crossroads (as was the custom) or drowned and therefore unrecovered   387 *for aye* forever   389 *the Morning's love* the hunter Cephalus, lover of Aurora (Ovid, *Metamorphoses*, VII; Bottom as Pyramus mistakenly refers to him at V.1.197 as *Shafalus*)   390 *forester* keeper of a royal park

    I am feared in field and town.

399
     Goblin, lead them up and down.

400
 Here comes one.
   Enter Lysander.

LYSANDER
 Where art thou, proud Demetrius? Speak thou now.

PUCK

402
 Here, villain, drawn and ready. Where art thou?

LYSANDER
 I will be with thee straight.

PUCK   Follow me then

404
 To plainer ground.   *[Exit Lysander.]*
   Enter Demetrius.

DEMETRIUS   Lysander, speak again!
 Thou runaway, thou coward, art thou fled?
 Speak! In some bush? Where dost thou hide thy head?

PUCK
 Thou coward, art thou bragging to the stars,
 Telling the bushes that thou look'st for wars,

409
 And wilt not come? Come, recreant! come, thou child!

410
 I'll whip thee with a rod. He is defiled
 That draws a sword on thee.

DEMETRIUS   Yea, art thou there?

PUCK
 Follow my voice. We'll try no manhood here. *Exeunt.*
  [Enter Lysander.]

LYSANDER
 He goes before me and still dares me on;
 When I come where he calls, then he is gone.
 The villain is much lighter-heeled than I.

---

399 *Goblin* (Puck presumably addresses himself) **402** *drawn* i.e., with sword drawn **404** *plainer* smoother, more open **404, 412 s.d.** *Exit Lysander, Enter Lysander* (Neither Q1 nor F indicates comings and goings for Lysander and Demetrius, as the action seems to imply, so most modern editors supply them. F includes a marginal s.d. – "shifting places" – which may indicate that Lysander and Demetrius remain onstage and grope in the "darkness.") **409** *recreant* traitor, coward (literally, "promise breaker")

I followed fast, but faster he did fly,
That fallen am I in dark uneven way,   417
And here will rest me.
    [Lies down.]   Come, thou gentle day.
For if but once thou show me thy gray light,
I'll find Demetrius and revenge this spite.   420
    [Sleeps.]
    [Enter] Robin [Puck] and Demetrius.

PUCK
Ho, ho, ho! Coward, why com'st thou not?

DEMETRIUS
Abide me, if thou dar'st; for well I wot   422
Thou runn'st before me, shifting every place,
And dar'st not stand nor look me in the face.
Where art thou now?

PUCK   Come hither. I am here.

DEMETRIUS
Nay then, thou mock'st me. Thou shalt buy this dear   426
If ever I thy face by daylight see.
Now go thy way. Faintness constraineth me
To measure out my length on this cold bed.   429
By day's approach look to be visited.   430
    [Lies down and sleeps.]
    Enter Helena.

HELENA
O weary night, O long and tedious night,
Abate thy hours. Shine comforts from the east,   432
That I may back to Athens by daylight
From these that my poor company detest;   434
And sleep, that sometimes shuts up sorrow's eye,
Steal me awhile from mine own company.
    Sleep.

---

417 *That* so that   422 *Abide* wait for; *wot* know   426 *buy this dear* pay
dearly for this (probably a form of *aby;* cf. III.2.175)   429 *measure out my
length* i.e., lie down   432 *Abate thy hours* shorten your time   434 *my poor
company detest* hate being with me

PUCK

> Yet but three? Come one more.
> Two of both kinds makes up four.

439   Here she comes, curst and sad.

440   Cupid is a knavish lad

> Thus to make poor females mad.

[Enter Hermia.]

HERMIA

> Never so weary, never so in woe,
>> Bedabbled with the dew, and torn with briers,

444   I can no further crawl, no further go,
>> My legs can keep no pace with my desires.

> Here will I rest me till the break of day.
> Heavens shield Lysander, if they mean a fray!

[Lies down and sleeps.]

PUCK

> On the ground
> Sleep sound.
> I'll apply

450

> To your eye,
> Gentle lover, remedy.

[Squeezes the herb onto Lysander's eyelids.]

> When thou wak'st,
> Thou tak'st
> True delight
> In the sight
> Of thy former lady's eye;
> And the country proverb known,
> That every man should take his own,
> In your waking shall be shown:

460

461

> Jack shall have Jill,
> Nought shall go ill,

---

439 *curst* out of sorts   **444** *go* walk   **461** *Jack, Jill* (generic names for "boy" and "girl")

The man shall have his mare again, and all shall be well.   463

[Exit.]

*

∾ **IV.1** *Enter [Titania,] Queen of Fairies, and [Bottom the] Clown and Fairies [Peaseblossom, Cobweb, Moth, Mustardseed, and others]; and the King [Oberon] behind them.*

TITANIA
  Come, sit thee down upon this flowery bed,
    While I thy amiable cheeks do coy,   2
  And stick musk roses in thy sleek smooth head,
    And kiss thy fair large ears, my gentle joy.
BOTTOM   Where's Peaseblossom?
PEASEBLOSSOM   Ready.
BOTTOM   Scratch my head, Peaseblossom. Where's Monsieur Cobweb?
COBWEB   Ready.
BOTTOM   Monsieur Cobweb, good monsieur, get you   10
your weapons in your hand, and kill me a red-hipped
humblebee on the top of a thistle; and, good monsieur,
bring me the honey bag. Do not fret yourself too much
in the action, monsieur; and, good monsieur, have a
care the honey bag break not. I would be loath to have
you overflowen with a honey bag, signor. Where's   16
Monsieur Mustardseed?
MUSTARDSEED   Ready.
BOTTOM   Give me your neaf, Monsieur Mustardseed.   19
Pray you, leave your curtsy, good monsieur.   20

---

463 *The man . . . well* (a proverb suggesting a happy ending); **s.d.** (F adds the s.d. "They sleepe all the Act," which may indicate that the four lovers remain asleep on the stage [1] as the action continues, [2] during an interval between Acts Three and Four, or [3] during the interval and through the ensuing action – suggested by F's "Sleepers lye still" at IV.1.100. See Note on the Text.)

IV.1   2 *amiable* lovable; *coy* caress   **16** *overflowen* flooded   **19** *neaf* fist (i.e., shake my hand)   **20** *leave your curtsy* don't be so formal, you can stop bowing now (a *curtsy* was any gesture of respect)

MUSTARDSEED   What's your will?

22 BOTTOM   Nothing, good monsieur, but to help Cavalery
Peaseblossom to scratch. I must to the barber's, monsieur; for methinks I am marvelous hairy about the
face, and I am such a tender ass, if my hair do but tickle
me, I must scratch.

TITANIA
What, wilt thou hear some music, my sweet love?

BOTTOM   I have a reasonable good ear in music. Let's
29 have the tongs and the bones.
[Music: Tongs, rural music.]

TITANIA
30 Or say, sweet love, what thou desirest to eat.

BOTTOM   Truly, a peck of provender. I could munch
your good dry oats. Methinks I have a great desire to a
33 bottle of hay. Good hay, sweet hay, hath no fellow.

TITANIA
I have a venturous fairy that shall seek
35 The squirrel's hoard, and fetch thee [   ] new nuts.

BOTTOM   I had rather have a handful or two of dried
peas. But I pray you, let none of your people stir me. I
38 have an exposition of sleep come upon me.

TITANIA
Sleep thou, and I will wind thee in my arms.
40 Fairies, be gone, and be always away.   [Exeunt Fairies.]
41 So doth the woodbine the sweet honeysuckle

22–23 *Cavalery Peaseblossom* (Bottom's error for *cavaliere,* an Italian title for a gallant. The early texts read "Cavalery Cobweb," the alliteration of which suggests that Shakespeare made an error: Cobweb has been sent on a mission, and Peaseblossom is the scratcher, l. 7. But Bottom himself may be confused, and may in fact say "Cavalery Cobweb.")   **29** *the tongs and the bones* (crude instruments: the tongs were struck like a triangle, while the bones were clappers held between the fingers)   **33** *bottle* small bundle   **35** *thee [   ] new nuts* (the defective meter indicates that the early texts omitted something from the line; editors have suggested "fetch thee thence" and "fetch thee off")   **38** *exposition* (Bottom's error for "disposition," inclination to)   **40** *be always away* i.e., get out and stay out   **41–42** *So . . . entwist* (the bindweed, or *woodbine,* twists to the right, the *honeysuckle* to the left, creating an inseparable tangle, as the syntax implies)

Gently entwist; the female ivy so
Enrings the barky fingers of the elm.
O, how I love thee! how I dote on thee!
    [They sleep.]
    Enter Robin Goodfellow [Puck].
OBERON   *[Advances.]*
    Welcome, good Robin. Seest thou this sweet sight?
    Her dotage now I do begin to pity,
    For, meeting her of late behind the wood,
    Seeking sweet favors for this hateful fool,   48
    I did upbraid her and fall out with her.
    For she his hairy temples then had rounded   50
    With coronet of fresh and fragrant flowers;
    And that same dew which sometime on the buds   52
    Was wont to swell, like round and orient pearls,   53
    Stood now within the pretty flowerets' eyes
    Like tears that did their own disgrace bewail.
    When I had at my pleasure taunted her,
    And she in mild terms begged my patience,
    I then did ask of her her changeling child;
    Which straight she gave me, and her fairy sent
    To bear him to my bower in fairyland.   60
    And now I have the boy, I will undo
    This hateful imperfection of her eyes.
    And, gentle Puck, take this transformèd scalp
    From off the head of this Athenian swain;   64
    That, he awaking when the other do,   65
    May all to Athens back again repair,
    And think no more of this night's accidents
    But as the fierce vexation of a dream.
    But first I will release the Fairy Queen.
        [He squeezes the herb onto her eyelids.]
            Be as thou wast wont to be;   70
            See as thou wast wont to see.

---

48 *favors* love gifts   **52** *sometime* formerly   **53** *Was wont to* used to; *orient*
lustrous (the rarest pearls were from the East)   **64** *swain* young man (the
word had lower-class associations)   **65** *other* others (common plural)

72   Dian's bud o'er Cupid's flower
                  Hath such force and blessèd power.
        Now, my Titania, wake you, my sweet queen.

TITANIA
    My Oberon, what visions have I seen!
    Methought I was enamored of an ass.

OBERON
    There lies your love.

TITANIA   How came these things to pass?
    O, how mine eyes do loathe his visage now!

OBERON
    Silence awhile. Robin, take off this head.
80   Titania, music call, and strike more dead
81   Than common sleep of all these five the sense.

TITANIA
    Music, ho, music! such as charmeth sleep.
      [Soft music.]

PUCK   *[Removes the ass head.]*
    Now, when thou wak'st, with thine own fool's eyes
      peep.

OBERON
    Sound, music!
      [Louder music.]
              Come, my queen, take hands with me.
85   And rock the ground whereon these sleepers be.
      [Dance.]
    Now thou and I are new in amity,
87   And will tomorrow midnight solemnly
88   Dance in Duke Theseus' house triumphantly
    And bless it to all fair prosperity.
90   There shall the pairs of faithful lovers be
    Wedded, with Theseus, all in jollity.

---

72 *Dian's bud* (perhaps *Agnus castus* or another plant associated with Diana and chastity; dramatically, it is the herbal antidote, mentioned at II.1.184, to *Cupid's flower,* the love-in-idleness, or pansy)   **81** *these five* Bottom and the lovers   **85** *rock the ground* (gently, as with a cradle; not in the modern sense)   **87** *solemnly* with ceremony (cf. *solemnities,* I.1.11)   **88** *triumphantly* in celebration

PUCK

    Fairy King, attend and mark:
    I do hear the morning lark.

OBERON

    Then, my queen, in silence sad   94
    Trip we after night's shade.   95
    We the globe can compass soon,
    Swifter than the wand'ring moon.

TITANIA

    Come, my lord, and in our flight
    Tell me how it came this night
    That I sleeping here was found   100
    With these mortals on the ground.   *Exeunt.*
 Wind horn. Enter Theseus and all his train [with
 Hippolyta and Egeus].

THESEUS

Go, one of you, find out the forester,
For now our observation is performed;   103
And since we have the vaward of the day,   104
My love shall hear the music of my hounds.
Uncouple in the western valley; let them go.   106
Dispatch, I say, and find the forester.   *[Exit Attendant.]*
We will, fair queen, up to the mountain's top
And mark the musical confusion
Of hounds and echo in conjunction.   110

HIPPOLYTA

I was with Hercules and Cadmus once   111
When in a wood of Crete they bayed the bear   112
With hounds of Sparta. Never did I hear   113
Such gallant chiding; for, besides the groves,   114
The skies, the fountains, every region near
Seemed all one mutual cry. I never heard

---

94 *sad* serious   95 *night's* (pronounced with two syllables: "nightes," the old possessive form)   103 *observation* observance (i.e., of the rite of May: I.1.167; IV.1.132)   104 *vaward . . . day* vanguard of the day, morning   106 *Uncouple* unleash (the pairs of *hounds*)   111 *Cadmus* the legendary founder of Thebes   112 *bayed* brought to bay, cornered   113 *hounds of Sparta* (a breed of dog famous in the ancient world)   114 *chiding* barking

So musical a discord, such sweet thunder.

THESEUS

My hounds are bred out of the Spartan kind:

119 So flewed, so sanded, and their heads are hung
120 With ears that sweep away the morning dew;
121 Crook-kneed, and dewlapped like Thessalian bulls;
122 Slow in pursuit, but matched in mouth like bells,
123 Each under each. A cry more tuneable

Was never holloed to nor cheered with horn

In Crete, in Sparta, nor in Thessaly.

126 Judge when you hear. But soft! What nymphs are these?

EGEUS

My lord, this is my daughter here asleep,

And this, Lysander, this Demetrius is,

This Helena, old Nedar's Helena.

130 I wonder of their being here together.

THESEUS

No doubt they rose up early to observe

The rite of May, and, hearing our intent,

133 Came here in grace of our solemnity.

But speak, Egeus. Is not this the day

That Hermia should give answer of her choice?

EGEUS

It is, my lord.

THESEUS

Go, bid the huntsmen wake them with their horns.

[Exit an Attendant.]

Shout within: they all start up. Wind horns.

138 Good morrow, friends. Saint Valentine is past:
139 Begin these wood birds but to couple now?

---

119 *So flewed, so sanded* i.e., resembling the Spartan dogs, with hanging chaps (*flewed*) and a sandy color **121** *dewlapped like Thessalian bulls* i.e., with large hanging flaps of skin beneath the throat **122–23** *matched . . . each* i.e., with harmonious voices differently pitched, from high to low **123** *cry* noise of the pack, hence the pack itself; *tuneable* in tune, musical **126** *soft* wait; *nymphs* woodland creatures, usually female **133** *in grace . . . solemnity* to honor our celebration **138–39** *Saint Valentine . . . now* (according to legend, birds mate on Saint Valentine's Day) **139** *couple* pair off

LYSANDER
  Pardon, my lord.   140
    [They kneel.]
THESEUS   I pray you all, stand up.
  I know you two are rival enemies.
  How comes this gentle concord in the world,
  That hatred is so far from jealousy   143
  To sleep by hate and fear no enmity?
LYSANDER
  My lord, I shall reply amazèdly,   145
  Half sleep, half waking; but as yet, I swear,
  I cannot truly say how I came here.
  But, as I think – for truly would I speak –
  And now I do bethink me, so it is,
  I came with Hermia hither. Our intent   150
  Was to be gone from Athens, where we might,   151
  Without the peril of the Athenian law –   152
EGEUS
  Enough, enough, my lord! you have enough.
  I beg the law, the law, upon his head.
  They would have stol'n away, they would, Demetrius,
  Thereby to have defeated you and me –   156
  You of your wife, and me of my consent,
  Of my consent that she should be your wife.
DEMETRIUS
  My lord, fair Helen told me of their stealth,
  Of this their purpose hither, to this wood,   160
  And I in fury hither followed them,
  Fair Helena in fancy following me.   162
  But, my good lord, I wot not by what power –   163
  But by some power it is – my love to Hermia,
  Melted as the snow, seems to me now
  As the remembrance of an idle gaud   166
  Which in my childhood I did dote upon,

---

143 *jealousy* suspicion 145 *amazèdly* confusedly 151 *where* wherever
152 *Without* outside 156 *defeated* (1) cheated, (2) deprived 162 *in fancy*
in love 163 *wot* know 166 *idle gaud* worthless trinket

168 And all the faith, the virtue of my heart,
The object and the pleasure of mine eye,
170 Is only Helena. To her, my lord,
Was I betrothed ere I saw Hermia,
172 But, like a sickness, did I loathe this food;
But, as in health, come to my natural taste,
Now I do wish it, love it, long for it,
And will for evermore be true to it.

THESEUS
Fair lovers, you are fortunately met.
Of this discourse we more will hear anon.
Egeus, I will overbear your will,
179 For in the temple, by and by, with us,
180 These couples shall eternally be knit;
181 And, for the morning now is something worn,
Our purposed hunting shall be set aside.
Away, with us to Athens! Three and three,
We'll hold a feast in great solemnity.
Come, Hippolyta.
                [Exeunt Theseus, Hippolyta, Egeus, and Lords.]

DEMETRIUS
These things seem small and undistinguishable,
Like far-off mountains turnèd into clouds.

HERMIA
188 Methinks I see these things with parted eye,
When everything seems double.

HELENA   So methinks;
190 And I have found Demetrius like a jewel,
Mine own, and not mine own.

DEMETRIUS   Are you sure
That we are awake? It seems to me
That yet we sleep, we dream. Do not you think
The duke was here and bid us follow him?

---

168 *virtue* power   172 *like a sickness* i.e., as in sickness   179 *by and by*
shortly   181 *for* because   188 *with parted eye* i.e., with the eyes not in focus
190–91 *And I . . . own* i.e., like a gem found by accident, and therefore not
really mine

HERMIA
  Yea, and my father.
HELENA   And Hippolyta.
LYSANDER
  And he did bid us follow to the temple.
DEMETRIUS
  Why then, we are awake. Let's follow him,
  And by the way let us recount our dreams.   *[Exeunt.]*
BOTTOM   *[Wakes.]* When my cue comes, call me, and I
  will answer. My next is "Most fair Pyramus." Hey-ho.   200
  Peter Quince? Flute the bellows mender? Snout the tin-
  ker? Starveling? God's my life! Stolen hence, and left   202
  me asleep? I have had a most rare vision. I have had a
  dream, past the wit of man to say what dream it was.
  Man is but an ass if he go about to expound this dream.
  Methought I was – there is no man can tell what.
  Methought I was, and methought I had – But man is
  but a patched fool if he will offer to say what   208
  methought I had. The eye of man hath not heard, the   209
  ear of man hath not seen, man's hand is not able to   210
  taste, his tongue to conceive, nor his heart to report
  what my dream was. I will get Peter Quince to write a
  ballet of this dream. It shall be called "Bottom's   213
  Dream," because it hath no bottom; and I will sing it in   214
  the latter end of our play, before the duke. Peradven-   215
  ture, to make it the more gracious, I shall sing it at her   216
  death.   *[Exit.]*

----

202 *God's my life* (a common oath, perhaps contracted from "God save my
life")   208 *a patched fool* i.e., a fool in motley   209–11 *The eye . . . report*
(Bottom's garbled version of I Corinthians 2:9–10: "But we preach as it is
written, things which eye hath not seen, and ear hath not heard, neither have
entered into man's mind, which things God hath prepared for them that love
him. But God hath opened them unto us by his spirit, for the spirit
searcheth all things, yea, the bottom of God's secrets." Some believe the last
phrase to be the source of Bottom's name.)   213 *ballet* ballad   214 *because
it hath no bottom* i.e., (1) because its meaning is unclear (he "can't get to the
bottom of it"), (2) because it is like a tangled skein of wool with no base or
bottom (a metaphor from weaving)   215–16 *Peradventure* perhaps   216–17
her death (probably Thisby's)

*

∾ **IV.2** *Enter Quince, Flute [with Snout and Starveling].*

QUINCE   Have you sent to Bottom's house? Is he come
    home yet?

STARVELING   He cannot be heard of. Out of doubt he is
4   transported.

FLUTE   If he come not, then the play is marred; it goes
    not forward, doth it?

QUINCE   It is not possible. You have not a man in all
    Athens able to discharge Pyramus but he.

9 FLUTE   No, he hath simply the best wit of any handicraft
10   man in Athens.

11 QUINCE   Yea, and the best person too, and he is a very
    paramour for a sweet voice.

FLUTE   You must say "paragon." A paramour is (God
14   bless us!) a thing of naught.
        Enter Snug the Joiner.

SNUG   Masters, the duke is coming from the temple, and
16   there is two or three lords and ladies more married. If
    our sport had gone forward, we had all been made
    men.

19 FLUTE   O sweet bully Bottom! Thus hath he lost six-
20   pence a day during his life. He could not have scaped
21   sixpence a day. An the duke had not given him sixpence
    a day for playing Pyramus, I'll be hanged! He would
    have deserved it. Sixpence a day in Pyramus, or noth-
    ing!
        Enter Bottom.

IV.2 Quince's house (?)   **4** *transported* carried off by spirits (see *translated*,
III.1.113–14)   **9** *wit* brains   **11** *person* figure, appearance   **14** *a thing of
naught* (1) a wicked thing (stronger than the modern "naughty"), (2) worth
nothing   **16–18** *If our sport . . . made men* i.e., if we had been able to perform our play, our fortunes would have been *made*   **19** *bully* jolly   **19–20**
sixpence a day i.e., a pension from the duke   **21** *An* if

BOTTOM   Where are these lads? Where are these hearts?   25

QUINCE   Bottom! O most courageous day! O most   26
happy hour!   27

BOTTOM   Masters, I am to discourse wonders, but ask   28
me not what. For if I tell you, I am not true Athenian.
I will tell you everything, right as it fell out.   30

QUINCE   Let us hear, sweet Bottom.

BOTTOM   Not a word of me. All that I will tell you is,   32
that the duke hath dined. Get your apparel together,
good strings to your beards, new ribbands to your   34
pumps; meet presently at the palace; every man look   35
o'er his part; for the short and the long is, our play is
preferred. In any case, let Thisby have clean linen; and   37
let not him that plays the lion pare his nails, for they
shall hang out for the lion's claws. And, most dear actors, eat no onions nor garlic, for we are to utter sweet   40
breath; and I do not doubt but to hear them say it is a
sweet comedy. No more words. Away, go, away!

[Exeunt.]

*

∾ **V.1** *Enter Theseus, Hippolyta, and Philostrate*
[with Lords and Attendants].

HIPPOLYTA

'Tis strange, my Theseus, that these lovers speak of.   1

THESEUS

More strange than true. I never may believe
These antique fables nor these fairy toys.   3
Lovers and madmen have such seething brains,

---

25 *hearts* good fellows   26 *courageous* brave, splendid (?) (perhaps auspi-
cious, lucky)   27 *happy* fortunate   28 *am to* have to   32 *word of* word out
of   34 *strings to your beards* i.e., to hold them on; *ribbands* (common spelling
of "ribbons")   35 *presently* right away   37 *preferred* recommended, chosen
    V.1 The duke's palace   1 *that* that which, what   3 *antique* (1) mad or
bizarre, "antic," (2) ancient, old; *fairy toys* i.e., foolish, supernatural stories
(*toys* are "trifles")

5   Such shaping fantasies, that apprehend
     More than cool reason ever comprehends.
     The lunatic, the lover, and the poet
8   Are of imagination all compact.
     One sees more devils than vast hell can hold:
10 That is the madman. The lover, all as frantic,
11 Sees Helen's beauty in a brow of Egypt.
     The poet's eye, in a fine frenzy rolling,
     Doth glance from heaven to earth, from earth to
       heaven,
14 And as imagination bodies forth
     The forms of things unknown, the poet's pen
     Turns them to shapes, and gives to airy nothing
     A local habitation and a name.
     Such tricks hath strong imagination
19 That, if it would but apprehend some joy,
20 It comprehends some bringer of that joy;
     Or in the night, imagining some fear,
     How easy is a bush supposed a bear!

HIPPOLYTA
     But all the story of the night told over,
24 And all their minds transfigured so together,
25 More witnesseth than fancy's images
26 And grows to something of great constancy;
27 But howsoever, strange and admirable.
     Enter Lovers: Lysander, Demetrius, Hermia, and
     Helena.

THESEUS
     Here come the lovers, full of joy and mirth.

---

5 *shaping fantasies* creative imaginations, powers of fantasy   **8** *of imagination all compact* composed entirely of imagination – i.e., without reason   **11** *Sees Helen's beauty . . . of Egypt* i.e., imagines that he sees female perfection (the Greek Helen was the ancient model of beauty) in the face of a gypsy   **14** *bodies forth* gives reality to, embodies   **19–20** *if . . . joy* i.e., if it wants to feel pleasure, it invents some imaginary source of that feeling   **24** *transfigured so together* so entirely changed all at once   **25** *More . . . images* speaks of more than mere figments of the imagination   **26** *constancy* certainty (because of the consistency of the evidence)   **27** *howsoever* in any case; *admirable* provoking wonder

Joy, gentle friends, joy and fresh days of love
Accompany your hearts!   30
LYSANDER   More than to us
Wait in your royal walks, your board, your bed!
THESEUS
Come now, what masques, what dances shall we have,   32
To wear away this long age of three hours
Between our aftersupper and bedtime?   34
Where is our usual manager of mirth?   35
What revels are in hand? Is there no play
To ease the anguish of a torturing hour?
Call Philostrate.   38
PHILOSTRATE   Here, mighty Theseus.
THESEUS
Say, what abridgment have you for this evening?   39
What masque? what music? How shall we beguile   40
The lazy time, if not with some delight?
PHILOSTRATE
There is a brief how many sports are ripe.   42
Make choice of which your highness will see first.
     [Gives a paper.]
THESEUS
"The battle with the Centaurs, to be sung   44
By an Athenian eunuch to the harp."
We'll none of that. That have I told my love
In glory of my kinsman Hercules.
"The riot of the tipsy Bacchanals,   48

---

32 *masques* courtly skits or pageants involving costumed, sometimes masked,
dancers 34 *aftersupper* light course finishing the evening meal 35 *manager
of mirth* supervisor of entertainments 38 *Philostrate* (Philostrate describes
the possible diversions only in the QQ texts; in F his part is assigned to
Egeus) 39 *abridgment* pastime (i.e., a diversion to "bridge" the hours between supper and bed) 42 *brief* list, memorandum; *sports are ripe* entertainments are prepared 44 *The battle . . . Centaurs* (a famous ancient
episode in which the Centaurs attempted to steal the bride of Pirithous,
Theseus's friend, during a wedding festival; in this version, as Theseus's response indicates, Hercules was a participant in the defense) 48–49 *The
riot . . . rage* (Ovid's story of Orpheus, dismembered by the Bacchantes;
Metamorphoses, XI)

Tearing the Thracian singer in their rage."
50 That is an old device, and it was played
When I from Thebes came last a conqueror.
52 "The thrice three Muses mourning for the death
Of Learning, late deceased in beggary."
That is some satire keen and critical,
55 Not sorting with a nuptial ceremony.
"A tedious brief scene of young Pyramus
And his love Thisby; very tragical mirth."
Merry and tragical? tedious and brief?
59 That is hot ice and wondrous strange snow.
60 How shall we find the concord of this discord?

PHILOSTRATE
A play there is, my lord, some ten words long,
Which is as brief as I have known a play;
But by ten words, my lord, it is too long,
Which makes it tedious. For in all the play
There is not one word apt, one player fitted.
And tragical, my noble lord, it is,
For Pyramus therein doth kill himself.
Which when I saw rehearsed, I must confess,
Made mine eyes water, but more merry tears
70 The passion of loud laughter never shed.

THESEUS
What are they that do play it?

PHILOSTRATE
Hardhanded men that work in Athens here,
Which never labored in their minds till now;
74 And now have toiled their unbreathed memories
75 With this same play, against your nuptial.

---

50 *device* show   **52–53** *The thrice . . . beggary* (apparently a poetic lament over the decline of learning and poetry; cf. Spenser's "The Teares of the Muses," 1591)   **55** *sorting with* appropriate to   **59** *strange snow* (perhaps a textual error; *hot ice* earlier in the line would seem to call for a similarly oxymoronic phrase, such as "scorching snow" or "sable snow")   **70** *passion* eruption (of powerful feeling)   **74** *unbreathed* unused, unexercised   **75** *against* in preparation for

THESEUS
  And we will hear it.
PHILOSTRATE   No, my noble lord,
  It is not for you. I have heard it over,
  And it is nothing, nothing in the world;
  Unless you can find sport in their intents,   79
  Extremely stretched and conned with cruel pain,   80
  To do you service.
THESEUS   I will hear that play,
  For never anything can be amiss
  When simpleness and duty tender it.   83
  Go bring them in; and take your places, ladies.

                        [Exit Philostrate.]

HIPPOLYTA
  I love not to see wretchedness o'ercharged,   85
  And duty in his service perishing.
THESEUS
  Why, gentle sweet, you shall see no such thing.
HIPPOLYTA
  He says they can do nothing in this kind.   88
THESEUS
  The kinder we, to give them thanks for nothing.
  Our sport shall be to take what they mistake,   90
  And what poor duty cannot do, noble respect   91
  Takes it in might, not merit.   92
  Where I have come, great clerks have purposèd   93
  To greet me with premeditated welcomes;
  Where I have seen them shiver and look pale,
  Make periods in the midst of sentences,
  Throttle their practiced accent in their fears,   97
  And, in conclusion, dumbly have broke off,

---

79 *intents* (refers both to their overtaxed intentions – *Extremely stretched* – and to their intended roles, which have been difficult to learn, *conned with cruel pain*)   **83** *simpleness* i.e., innocent good will   **85** *o'ercharged* required to do too much   **88** *in this kind* of this sort   **91** *noble respect* aristocratic sensitivity   **92** *Takes . . . merit* i.e., takes the intention for the actual performance   **93** *great clerks* important scholars   **97** *practiced accent* rehearsed manner

Not paying me a welcome. Trust me, sweet,
100 Out of this silence yet I picked a welcome,
And in the modesty of fearful duty
I read as much as from the rattling tongue
103 Of saucy and audacious eloquence.
Love, therefore, and tongue-tied simplicity
105 In least speak most, to my capacity.
     [Enter Philostrate.]

PHILOSTRATE
106 So please your grace the Prologue is addressed.

THESEUS
107 Let him approach.
     [Flourish trumpets.] Enter the Prologue [Quince].

PROLOGUE
108 If we offend, it is with our good will.
That you should think, we come not to offend
110 But with good will. To show our simple skill,
That is the true beginning of our end.
Consider then, we come but in despite.
We do not come, as minding to content you,
Our true intent is. All for your delight,
We are not here. That you should here repent you,
The actors are at hand: and, by their show,
You shall know all, that you are like to know.

118 THESEUS   This fellow doth not stand upon points.
119 LYSANDER   He hath rid his prologue like a rough colt; he
120 knows not the stop. A good moral, my lord: it is not
enough to speak, but to speak true.

---

103 *saucy* impudent   105 *In least* in speaking least; *to my capacity* to my way
of thinking   106 *addressed* ready   107 s.d. (F specifies the trumpet flourish
and identifies Quince as the speaker of the prologue)   108–17 (the indiscriminate punctuation – noted by Theseus in l. 118 – was a standard comic
routine and source of laughter)   118 *doth not stand upon points* i.e., doesn't
worry about (1) punctuation, (2) subtleties   119 *rough* unbroken   119–20
he . . . stop i.e., the speech is running away with the speaker; *stop* plays on (1)
the checking of a horse in full gallop, (2) a period

HIPPOLYTA   Indeed he hath played on this prologue like a
   child on a recorder – a sound, but not in government.   123
THESEUS   His speech was like a tangled chain; nothing
   impaired, but all disordered. Who is next?

   Enter Pyramus and Thisby, and Wall and Moonshine
   and Lion.

PROLOGUE
   Gentles, perchance you wonder at this show,
      But wonder on, till truth make all things plain.
   This man is Pyramus, if you would know;
      This beauteous lady Thisby is certain.   129
   This man, with lime and roughcast, doth present   130
      Wall, that vile Wall which did these lovers sunder;
   And through Wall's chink, poor souls, they are content
      To whisper. At the which let no man wonder.
   This man, with lantern, dog, and bush of thorn,   134
      Presenteth Moonshine. For, if you will know,
   By moonshine did these lovers think no scorn
      To meet at Ninus' tomb, there, there to woo.
   This grisly beast (which Lion hight by name)   138
   The trusty Thisby, coming first by night,
   Did scare away, or rather did affright;   140
   And as she fled, her mantle she did fall,   141
      Which Lion vile with bloody mouth did stain.
   Anon comes Pyramus, sweet youth and tall,   143
      And finds his trusty Thisby's mantle slain;
   Whereat, with blade, with bloody blameful blade,
      He bravely broached his boiling bloody breast.   146
   And Thisby, tarrying in mulberry shade,
      His dagger drew, and died. For all the rest,

---

123 *recorder* flutelike instrument; *in government* under control   **129** *certain*
(the accent on the second syllable, as required by the rhyme, was already archaic in the 1590s)   **134** *lantern . . . thorn* (see III.1.55–56)   **138** *hight* is
called (already archaic in the 1590s)   **141** *fall* let fall   **143** *tall* brave, hand-
some (as well as referring to height)   **146** *bravely broached . . . breast* (here
and below Shakespeare mocks the extravagant alliteration of old-fashioned
plays)

Let Lion, Moonshine, Wall, and lovers twain
150   At large discourse while here they do remain.
THESEUS   I wonder if the lion be to speak.
DEMETRIUS   No wonder, my lord. One lion may, when
many asses do.   *Exit [Prologue, with Pyramus,] Lion,*
Thisby, and Moonshine.

WALL
154   In this same interlude it doth befall
155   That I, one Snout by name, present a wall;
And such a wall, as I would have you think,
157   That had in it a crannied hole or chink,
Through which the lovers, Pyramus and Thisby,
Did whisper often, very secretly.
160   This loam, this roughcast, and this stone doth show
That I am that same wall: the truth is so.
162   And this the cranny is, right and sinister,
Through which the fearful lovers are to whisper.
THESEUS   Would you desire lime and hair to speak better?
166   DEMETRIUS   It is the wittiest partition that ever I heard
discourse, my lord.
        [Enter Pyramus.]
THESEUS   Pyramus draws near the wall. Silence!
PYRAMUS
O grim-looked night, O night with hue so black,
170   O night, which ever art when day is not!
O night, O night, alack, alack, alack,
I fear my Thisby's promise is forgot.
And thou, O wall, O sweet, O lovely wall,
That stand'st between her father's ground and mine,
Thou wall, O wall, O sweet and lovely wall,
Show me thy chink, to blink through with mine eyne.

---

150 *at large* at length   154 *interlude* (old-fashioned term for a play)   155
present play the role of, represent   157 *chink* (a slang term for "vagina" or
"anus," and part of a network of obscene jokes running through the mechanicals' play)   162 *sinister* left (the cranny is horizontal, right and left)
166 *partition* (1) wall, (2) section of an oration

[Wall holds up his fingers.]
Thanks, courteous wall. Jove shield thee well for this.
  But what see I? No Thisby do I see.
O wicked wall, through whom I see no bliss,
  Cursed be thy stones for thus deceiving me!   180

THESEUS   The wall, methinks, being sensible, should   181
curse again.

PYRAMUS   No, in truth, sir, he should not. "Deceiving
me" is Thisby's cue. She is to enter now, and I am to spy
her through the wall. You shall see it will fall pat as I
told you. Yonder she comes.
  Enter Thisby.

THISBY
O wall, full often hast thou heard my moans
  For parting my fair Pyramus and me.
My cherry lips have often kissed thy stones,
  Thy stones with lime and hair knit up in thee.   *190*

PYRAMUS
I see a voice. Now will I to the chink,
  To spy an I can hear my Thisby's face.   192
Thisby!

THISBY   My love! thou art my love, I think.

PYRAMUS
Think what thou wilt, I am thy lover's grace;   194
And, like Limander, am I trusty still.   195

THISBY
And I, like Helen, till the Fates me kill.

PYRAMUS
Not Shafalus to Procrus was so true.

---

180 *stones* the components of the wall (but with a pun on "testicles," one of
a string of obscene jokes: cf. *hair* at l. 190 and *hole* at l. 199)   **181** *sensible* ca-
pable of perception   **192** *an* if   **194** *thy lover's grace* i.e., thy gracious lover
195–97 *Limander . . . Procrus* (there is much intentional confusion here,
with mixed-up stories and inappropriate examples: *Limander* is Bottom's
error for Leander, from Marlowe's poem "Hero and Leander"; *Helen* is not
the lover of Limander/Leander, and she is hardly *trusty*; *Shafalus* and *Procrus*
are slips for Cephalus and Procris, another pair of tragic lovers)

THISBY
    As Shafalus to Procrus, I to you.

PYRAMUS
    O, kiss me through the hole of this vile wall!

THISBY
200   I kiss the wall's hole, not your lips at all.

PYRAMUS
    Wilt thou at Ninny's tomb meet me straightway?

THISBY
202   'Tide life, 'tide death, I come without delay.

                [Exeunt Pyramus and Thisby.]

WALL
    Thus have I, Wall, my part dischargèd so;
    And, being done, thus Wall away doth go.   *[Exit.]*

205 THESEUS Now is the mural down between the two
    neighbors.

DEMETRIUS No remedy, my lord, when walls are so will-
208 ful to hear without warning.

HIPPOLYTA This is the silliest stuff that ever I heard.

210 THESEUS The best in this kind are but shadows, and the
    worst are no worse, if imagination amend them.

HIPPOLYTA It must be your imagination then, and not
    theirs.

THESEUS If we imagine no worse of them than they of
    themselves, they may pass for excellent men. Here
    come two noble beasts in, a man and a lion.

    Enter Lion and Moonshine.

LION
    You, ladies, you whose gentle hearts do fear
      The smallest monstrous mouse that creeps on floor,
    May now perchance both quake and tremble here,
220   When lion rough in wildest rage doth roar.

---

202 *'Tide . . . death* come (betide) life, come death 205 *mural* wall (a famous textual problem: Q1 reads "Now is the moon used"; F reads "Now is
the morall down"; the emendation here was first proposed by Alexander
Pope) 208 *to hear without warning* i.e., without alerting the lovers' families
(a joke on walls having ears) 210 *best . . . shadows* best of this sort – i.e., the
best actors – aren't real anyway (*shadows* was a conventional term for "players")

Then know that I, as Snug the joiner, am   221
A lion fell, nor else no lion's dam;   222
For if I should as lion come in strife
Into this place, 'twere pity on my life.   224

THESEUS A very gentle beast, and of a good conscience. 225

DEMETRIUS The very best at a beast, my lord, that e'er I 226
saw.

LYSANDER This lion is a very fox for his valor.   228

THESEUS True, and a goose for his discretion.

DEMETRIUS Not so, my lord, for his valor cannot carry   230
his discretion, and the fox carries the goose.

THESEUS His discretion, I am sure, cannot carry his
valor, for the goose carries not the fox. It is well. Leave
it to his discretion, and let us listen to the moon.

MOON
This lanthorn doth the hornèd moon present –   235

DEMETRIUS He should have worn the horns on his head.   236

THESEUS He is no crescent, and his horns are invisible 237
within the circumference.

MOON
This lanthorn doth the hornèd moon present.
Myself the man i' th' moon do seem to be.   240

THESEUS This is the greatest error of all the rest. The
man should be put into the lanthorn. How is it else the
man i' th' moon?

221–22 *I . . . dam* (Snug scrupulously distinguishes between an actual lion and his impersonation of a lion, in light of the concerns expressed during the rehearsal) 222 *lion fell* (1) fierce lion, (2) lion's skin 224 *'twere pity on my life* i.e., I'd sooner die than frighten you into thinking I am really a lion 225 *gentle* courteous, well-mannered 226 *best at a beast* (a pun based on similar pronunciation: the wordplay introduces a series of jests among the spectators – involving *discretion, horns,* and *snuff* – amounting to a kind of verbal one-upmanship) 228 *This lion . . . valor* (alluding to the proverb "Discretion is the better part of valor"; the lion was known for courage, the fox for cunning [*discretion*], and the *goose* [l.229] for stupidity) 235 *lanthorn* lantern (pronounced "lant-horn" or "lantern") 236 *on his head* (*horns* on the forehead were the sign of a cuckold, a betrayed husband) 237 *no crescent* not waxing or growing (Starveling is probably thin)

244 DEMETRIUS   He dares not come there, for the candle; for
245   you see it is already in snuff.

HIPPOLYTA   I am aweary of this moon. Would he would
   change!

THESEUS   It appears, by his small light of discretion, that
   he is in the wane; but yet, in courtesy, in all reason, we
250   must stay the time.

LYSANDER   Proceed, Moon.

MOON   All that I have to say is to tell you that the lanthorn is the moon; I, the man i' th' moon; this thornbush, my thornbush; and this dog, my dog.

DEMETRIUS   Why, all these should be in the lanthorn, for
   all these are in the moon. But silence: here comes
   Thisby.

   Enter Thisby.

THISBY
   This is old Ninny's tomb. Where is my love?

LION   O!   *[The Lion roars. Thisby runs off.]*
260 DEMETRIUS   Well roared, Lion.

THESEUS   Well run, Thisby.

HIPPOLYTA   Well shone, Moon. Truly, the moon shines
   with a good grace.

                    [The Lion tears Thisby's mantle, and exits.]
264 THESEUS   Well moused, Lion.

DEMETRIUS   And then came Pyramus.

LYSANDER   And so the lion vanished.

   Enter Pyramus.

PYRAMUS
   Sweet moon, I thank thee for thy sunny beams;
      I thank thee, moon, for shining now so bright;
   For, by thy gracious, golden, glittering gleams,
270   I trust to take of truest Thisby sight.

---

244 *for the candle* for fear of the burning candle   **245** *in snuff* (1) in need of
snuffing, (2) in a huff, fit of anger (Starveling may have become impatient
with the interruptions of the spectators)   **264** *Well moused* i.e., the lion with
the mantle in his mouth is like a cat with a mouse

But stay: O spite!   271
But mark, poor knight,
What dreadful dole is here?   273
Eyes, do you see?
How can it be?
O dainty duck, O dear!
Thy mantle good,
What, stained with blood?
Approach, ye Furies fell!   279
O Fates, come, come,   280
Cut thread and thrum,   281
Quail, crush, conclude, and quell!   282

Furies
Clotho→spun
Lachesis→measure
Atropos→cut

THESEUS   This passion, and the death of a dear friend,   283
would go near to make a man look sad.

HIPPOLYTA   Beshrew my heart but I pity the man.   285

PYRAMUS
O, wherefore, Nature, didst thou lions frame?
Since lion vile hath here deflowered my dear;   287
Which is – no, no! – which was the fairest dame
That lived, that loved, that liked, that looked with cheer.
Come, tears, confound,   290
Out, sword, and wound
The pap of Pyramus: 292
Ay, that left pap
Where heart doth hop.

[Stabs himself.]
Thus die I, thus, thus, thus.
Now am I dead,
Now am I fled,
My soul is in the sky.

---

271 *spite* bad fortune   273 *dole* cause of sadness   279 *Furies fell* fierce
agents of fate (invoked in imitation of Senecan tragedy)   281 *thrum* the end
of the weaver's thread left attached to the loom after the web was cut away
(Bottom's shorthand for "finish the job")   282 *Quail* overpower; *quell* kill
283–84 *This passion . . . sad* i.e., this breast-beating by itself isn't emotionally
touching   285 *Beshrew my heart* (a mild curse or oath – "Damned if I don't
feel pity")   287 *deflowered* attacked   292 *pap* breast

Tongue, lose thy light,
300   Moon, take thy flight. *[Exit Moonshine.]*
Now die, die, die, die, die.

[Dies.]

302 DEMETRIUS   No die, but an ace, for him! for he is but one.

LYSANDER   Less than an ace, man; for he is dead, he is
nothing.

THESEUS   With the help of a surgeon he might yet re-
cover, and prove an ass.

HIPPOLYTA   How chance Moonshine is gone before
Thisby comes back and finds her lover?

[Enter Thisby.]

THESEUS   She will find him by starlight. Here she comes,
310   and her passion ends the play.

HIPPOLYTA   Methinks she should not use a long one for
such a Pyramus. I hope she will be brief.

DEMETRIUS   A mote will turn the balance, which Pyramus, which Thisby, is the better: he for a man, God
315   warrant us; she for a woman, God bless us!

LYSANDER   She hath spied him already with those sweet
eyes.

318 DEMETRIUS   And thus she means, videlicet:

THISBY

Asleep, my love?
320   What, dead, my dove?
O Pyramus, arise!
Speak, speak. Quite dumb?
Dead, dead? A tomb
Must cover thy sweet eyes.
These lily lips,
This cherry nose,
These yellow cowslip cheeks,

---

302 *ace* the one-spot on a die (with a pun on *ass* in l. 306); *one* (pun on
"unique" and "one man")   310 *passion* emotional speech   315 *warrant* protect, save   318 *means* (1) moans, laments (an Anglo-Saxon form), (2) lodges
a complaint; *videlicet* to wit, as you see

       Are gone, are gone.
       Lovers, make moan.
       His eyes were green as leeks.   330
         O Sisters Three,   331
         Come, come to me,
       With hands as pale as milk;
         Lay them in gore,
         Since you have shore   335
       With shears his thread of silk.
         Tongue, not a word.
         Come, trusty sword,
       Come, blade, my breast imbrue!   339
[Stabs herself.]
         And farewell, friends.   340
         Thus Thisby ends.
       Adieu, adieu, adieu.
[Dies.]
[Enter Lion, Moonshine, and Wall.]

THESEUS   Moonshine and Lion are left to bury the dead.

DEMETRIUS   Ay, and Wall too.

LION   No, I assure you; the wall is down that parted their   345
fathers. Will it please you to see the epilogue, or to hear
a Bergomask dance between two of our company?   347

THESEUS   No epilogue, I pray you; for your play needs
no excuse. Never excuse, for when the players are all
dead, there need none to be blamed. Marry, if he that   350
writ it had played Pyramus and hanged himself in   351
Thisby's garter, it would have been a fine tragedy; and
so it is truly, and very notably discharged. But, come,
your Bergomask. Let your epilogue alone.

---

331 *Sisters Three* the Fates   **335** *shore* (archaic form of "shorn" – for comic effect)   **339** *imbrue* (1) stain with blood, (2) plunge into   **345** *LION* (F assigns this speech to Bottom)   **347** *Bergomask dance* rustic dance (originally Italian, from Bergamo; plays in the public theaters – comedies and tragedies – were often followed by jigs or rousing dances)   **351–52** *hanged . . . garter* (condescending description of suicide; from a proverbial phrase, "To hang himself in his own garters")

[A dance.]

355 The iron tongue of midnight hath told twelve.
Lovers, to bed; 'tis almost fairy time.
I fear we shall outsleep the coming morn
358 As much as we this night have overwatched.
This palpable gross play hath well beguiled
360 The heavy gait of night. Sweet friends, to bed.
A fortnight hold we this solemnity
In nightly revels and new jollity.   *Exeunt.*
    Enter Puck [with a broom].

PUCK
          Now the hungry lion roars,
              And the wolf behowls the moon,
          Whilst the heavy plowman snores,
366   All with weary task fordone.
367   Now the wasted brands do glow,
              Whilst the screech owl, screeching loud,
          Puts the wretch that lies in woe
370   In remembrance of a shroud.
          Now it is the time of night
              That the graves, all gaping wide,
373   Every one lets forth his sprite,
              In the churchway paths to glide.
          And we fairies, that do run
376   By the triple Hecate's team
          From the presence of the sun,
              Following darkness like a dream,
379   Now are frolic. Not a mouse
380   Shall disturb this hallowed house.
          I am sent, with broom, before,

---

355 *told* counted (including the sense of "tolled")   358 *overwatched* stayed up too late   360 *heavy gait* plodding pace   366 *fordone* undone, exhausted 367 *brands* coals   373 *Every one* each grave (l. 372); *his* its; *sprite* spirit, ghost 376 *triple Hecate's team* i.e., the dragons pulling the chariot of the goddess known in the underworld as Hecate, on earth as Diana, and in the sky as Cynthia or Luna or Phoebe   379 *frolic* merry, frolicsome

To sweep the dust behind the door.   382
Enter King and Queen of Fairies, with all their train.

OBERON

Through the house give glimmering light,
    By the dead and drowsy fire;
Every elf and fairy sprite
    Hop as light as bird from brier;
And this ditty, after me,
Sing, and dance it trippingly.

TITANIA

First rehearse your song by rote,
To each word a warbling note.   390
Hand in hand with fairy grace
Will we sing and bless this place.   392
   [Song and dance.]

OBERON

Now until the break of day
Through this house each fairy stray.
To the best bridebed will we,
Which by us shall blessèd be,
And the issue there create
Ever shall be fortunate.
So shall all the couples three
Ever true in loving be,   400
And the blots of Nature's hand
Shall not in their issue stand.
Never mole, harelip, nor scar,
Nor mark prodigious such as are   404
Despisèd in nativity
Shall upon their children be.
With this field dew consecrate   407

---

382 *behind the door* from behind the door (in folklore Puck was traditionally represented with broom and candle, signifying his role as housekeeper)   **392 s.d.** *Song and dance* (the song may be lost, or *Song* may refer to Oberon's verses that follow; headed "The Song" in F)   **404** *mark prodigious* ominous birthmark   **407** *field dew consecrate* (the field dew, blessed, serves as a kind of fairy holy water)

Every fairy take his gait,
And each several chamber bless
410 Through this palace with sweet peace.
And the owner of it blest
Ever shall in safety rest.
Trip away, make no stay,
Meet me all by break of day.
Exeunt [all but Puck].

PUCK
415 If we shadows have offended,
Think but this, and all is mended –
That you have but slumbered here
While these visions did appear.
419 And this weak and idle theme,
420 No more yielding but a dream,
421 Gentles, do not reprehend.
If you pardon, we will mend.
And, as I am an honest Puck,
If we have unearnèd luck
425 Now to scape the serpent's tongue,
We will make amends ere long;
Else the Puck a liar call.
So, good night unto you all.
429 Give me your hands, if we be friends,
430 And Robin shall restore amends. *[Exit.]*

---

415 *shadows* (1) spirits, (2) actors (an Elizabethan term) **419** *idle* foolish
420 *No more yielding but* yielding no more than **421** *reprehend* complain,
blame us **425** *scape* escape; *serpent's tongue* i.e., hissing **429** *Give . . . hands*
i.e., applaud for us